Naked
in the
Boardroom

A CEO BARES HER SECRETS SO YOU
CAN TRANSFORM YOUR CAREER

Robin Wolaner

A FIRESIDE BOOK
Published by Simon & Schuster

New York London Toronto Sydney

 FIRESIDE
Rockefeller Center
1230 Avenue of the Americas
New York, NY 10020

This Fireside Edition 2006

FIRESIDE and colophon are registered trademarks
of Simon & Schuster, Inc.

For information about special discounts for bulk purchases,
please contact Simon & Schuster Special Sales at
1-800-456-6798 or business@simonandschuster.com.

Designed by Ruth Lee-Mui

Manufactured in the United States of America

10 9 8 7 6 5 4 3 2 1

The Library of Congress has cataloged the hardcover edition as follows:

Wolaner, Robin.
    Naked in the boardroom: a CEO bares her secrets so you can
transform your career / Robin Wolaner.
        p. cm.
    "A Fireside book."
    1. Women executives—United States. 2. Women chief executive
officers—Training of—United States. 3. Women executives—Training
of—United States. 4. Industrial management—Vocational guidance—
United States. 5. Career development—United States. I. Title.

    HD6054.4.U6W65 2005
    650.1'3'082—dc22
                                                        2004057140
    ISBN-13: 978-0-7432-6227-9
    ISBN-10:   0-7432-6227-1
    ISBN-13: 978-0-7432-8284-0 (Pbk)
    ISBN-10:   0-7432-8284-1 (Pbk)

For Terry David Castleman and Bonnie Lee Castleman,
my most successful start-ups (and joint ventures)

In loving memory of

PAULA M. SIEGEL

This would be a better book,
and a better world, if Paula were still here.

CONTENTS

Naked
in the
Boardroom

MY MOTHER HATES THE WORD "NAKED" IN THIS BOOK'S title. One of my first business partners said, *"Naked in the boardroom? Well, you have always disarmed and then dismantled any man you were near, not the other way around."*

I don't mean it literally, Mom. And I'm glad my partner thought I was always in control. But what I mean is this: Getting naked is another term for getting real.

Naked in the Boardroom began as a letter to my daughter, Bonnie, when she was four. I was thinking about what her working life would be like as a woman, and how much had (and hadn't) changed since I began my career in the 1970s. But by the time I actually started writing this book, I realized that maybe my ambitions were for a larger audience: women like those I've met all through my career, who hunger for other women's hard-earned wisdom.

While today you enter the workforce believing that you

can have any position to which you aspire, you are still told to put on a business face, to make decisions based on analysis instead of personal beliefs and gut instincts, and, especially, to leave your emotions behind when you enter the office. Let's face it: The message is that to succeed, you should be more like men.

That's wrong.

Perhaps I'm comfortable with "naked" because my first job was at *Penthouse*. I am happy to report that the editorial and publishing employees were clothed, but getting naked is one reason why I succeeded in business. I showed my feelings and even vulnerability in the workplace. I was sensitive to the people with whom I worked. The lessons I learned in business all point to one broad truth: Success follows when you use what you've got. You will succeed because of, not in spite of, your personal traits. The trick is to make your aptitude and flair work for you in a style that is uniquely yours. Maybe I'm a cockeyed optimist, but I think the last decade of changes in business tilted the balance in our favor. Business moves faster, and that means that developing your gut instincts really pays off. Which gender is known for intuition? The biggest growth companies are in the information business: Who's better at getting, and sharing, information—men or women?

Men can be good at these.

Women are better.

Although much comes naturally, this book is intended to help you realize your particular strengths, to develop your ability to hear messages from your gut, and to shape your skills in listening, decision making, and negotiating—all essential to your career regardless of your seniority or industry. Each chapter is devoted to a specific business theme, accompanied by "take-away" sections filled with easily digested tips on specific career topics.

Kamala Harris, California's first African-American female district attorney, was told by her mother (a noted doctor), "It's great to be the first, you'll be the first at a lot of things, just make a path for others so you're not the last."

As part of a generation of women who were firsts, I think of Dr. Harris's words a lot. I was the youngest publisher of a national magazine in 1982, then the first entrepreneur that Time Inc. funded in a joint-venture start-up. In 1993, I was Time Warner's first divisional CEO to get pregnant. Then, I became a top executive at CNET, one of the first Internet companies to go public. There I suddenly found myself an elder stateswoman to young people who would ask me to be their mentor, to help them form a plan to succeed in work, in timing their families, in balance. In the hundreds of conversations I've had with women on the cusp of greatness—whether over late-night pizza or waiting at crowded airport gates—I've always ended up saying the same thing in different ways: Business is personal. Every necessary decision-making tool is already inside you—your experience, brain, and gut will tell you what to do, if you can access their messages. This is a skill that can be honed, and this book—and taking on the challenges presented to you—will show you how to do just that.

Most of the women I interviewed for this book, women who became CEOs and who were willing to get down and dirty, share my desire to help our female successors have it easier than we did. We hope that the next generation of businesswomen can learn from how we've grappled with real-life issues: hiring, firing (and getting hired and, er, fired), sexuality in the office, overt and covert discrimination, negotiating, recovering from a mistake. Few of these lessons come easily; indeed, I've learned as much, if not more, from mistakes and scoundrels over time as I have from easy decisions and heroes. My best mentors were the antimentors, whose examples I vowed to avoid.

Women in business today will far exceed the successes of the previous generation's women if they can just be themselves—be real—at work. This book will tell you how to be who you are and make it work for you. And you can keep your clothes on.

ONE

Hey Carly, It's Different Being a Woman

WHEN CARLY FIORINA WAS NAMED CEO OF HEWLETT-Packard, her insistence that being female was not part of her success story struck every woman I know as either delusional or a lie. Maybe now that Carly's been fired she feels differently.

NAKED TRUTH # 1

Sometimes it's better to be female in business, sometimes it's worse, but it's rarely the same.

If you believe business is the same for men and women, you either believe that:

- men and women are the same and gender differences are random, or

- psychological and biological influences are irrelevant in the workplace.

If the former, you and I have grown up in a different world. If the latter, perhaps you are male?

I began my career in the quintessentially female job of the seventies: as a secretary. I was lucky enough to be at a growing magazine company, where I was made a copywriter, then editor. I later moved to a job as editor of a trade magazine for people in the newsstand industry—the most male segment of magazine publishing. I wrote about a new magazine called *Runner's World,* and the founder offered to move me to California to launch it on newsstands nationally. My knowledge of magazine circulation, burnished during a stint working for a publishing consultant, led me to a position as general manager of *Mother Jones,* a nonprofit magazine that depended heavily on circulation (as opposed to advertising) revenue. I became publisher and stayed at *Mother Jones* for five years, then my longest tenure by a factor of four. To supplement my meager salary at *Mother Jones* I began teaching at the Radcliffe Publishing Course, which focused on magazine start-ups. In 1986 I had my own idea for a start-up, and raised $5 million from Time Inc. for a joint venture that launched *Parenting* magazine, one of the most successful new magazines of the last twenty years. After selling my interest to Time, I spent five years as an executive there, responsible for magazine development and their West Coast lifestyle publishing company, Sunset. After departing there in 1996 I became an executive at CNET, one of the first Internet companies to go public, and remained there through the tech-stock bubble and beyond, until leaving to write this book.

Sounds pretty businesslike and gender neutral, doesn't it? Yet being female affected almost every aspect of my career, for better (mostly) and worse. The founder of *Runner's World* hired me despite my lack of experience, largely because he thought a cute twenty-three-year-old would get outsize attention in the newsstand distribution world (and I did). The publishing consultant who taught me magazine economics also taught me never again to sleep with my boss. My motivation for leaving *Mother Jones* was to earn enough money to support my bankrupt new husband; the idea for *Parenting* occurred to me largely because I was considering getting pregnant.

NAKED TRUTH #2

Business is personal.

To write this book I interviewed dozens of women who'd reached CEO positions and two at the "C" level (chief, reporting to the CEO) in major companies. All achieved success in the business world almost unknown to previous generations. Each one cited romance, family, and relationship milestones alongside education, achievement, and finances. Read Jack Welch's first autobiography, *Straight from the Gut*, if you harbor the illusion that men see the world similarly. His marriages get a few nonreflective lines each and his philandering none at all. The women I interviewed eagerly recounted mistakes along with triumphs. I've tried to do the same.

There are two types of business books for women. (Reminds me of a friend's comment: "There are two types of people in the world: those who believe there are two types of people and those who don't.") The first type of book advises you to try to be like a man to succeed, which includes keeping your emotions out of the workplace. This book is the second type, which avers that a healthy leader recognizes, and responds to, the emotions involved in decision making and business relationships. Pretending to see logic in your boss's petulant behavior when you pay attention to his business rival doesn't make it go away. Realizing that he is behaving like your high school boyfriend—and treating him accordingly—just might.

NAKED TRUTH #3

Don't meet with a male colleague in a hotel room or private residence. Intentions may be innocent, but shit happens.

I'd had almost no social life in my first year postcollege, so attending business conventions was exciting instead of the chore it later became. However, the flirtatious atmosphere at conventions led to one encounter that was emotionally searing.

A man well respected and extremely powerful in his industry, who happened to be a seemingly proper married friend of my aunt and uncle, left the pool in Hilton Head at the same time as I did one afternoon. We walked back toward the villas that the conference attendees were all staying in together. I was chatting with him about my job, and he invited me into his villa for a soda. All was quite innocent as we sat in the living room and talked for a half hour about business.

When I needed to leave to go prepare for the dinner, he walked me to the door and said, "I am surprised that you would trust me enough to come to my hotel room." I said, breezily, "Oh, as long as you're walking me to the door and not the bedroom, I know it's okay." At which point he threw me over his shoulder and carried me into a small room nearby. I was laughing, figuring it was a joke, when I realized he was serious. Despite my tearful protests, only the Danskin leotard I was wearing instead of a bikini prevented him from raping me. Finally, he gave up and I fled.

Although my feminism makes me hesitate to take any blame for this tawdry episode, even at the time I knew I wasn't blameless. I had found him attractive, and probably would have been receptive if he'd been less of a lunatic. A man of his generation could probably be forgiven for misreading a woman's intent in visiting his villa in a bathing suit (and cover-up). Even after this terrifying event I sought him out at the dance that evening to demonstrate my lack of hard feelings, as I was afraid that if he wanted revenge he could keep me from getting ahead in the publishing industry. I was twenty-three.

At the next convention, he had stationed himself alone at a table in the bar, facing the corridor I needed to walk through to get to my room. I walked slowly until out of his sight, and then ran down the hall. I told several of my male friends about this; I was not sure they believed me until I learned that this same executive spent an evening bragging about his success with a model. He told his dinner guests that "when women say no they usually want it." Nat Lehrman, then the publisher of *Playboy*, told him, "Robin is our friend, and you keep your distance." With that comment, Nat made it clear that not all men need to force themselves, and he earned my undying gratitude. (A less chivalrous friend suggested I do a commercial for Danskin.)

The Hilton Head incident caused me to question my judgment and fear for my future. Now that I can be less emotional about it, I realize that the biggest negative consequence was that I had put myself in a situation that eliminated a potentially valuable industry contact. At the time, however, I thought I was incapable of working safely with men. If I had given in to that questioning and fear, you wouldn't be reading this book. Putting a continent between me and this man felt like a good decision, and an opportunity quickly came along.

I flew to San Francisco in July 1977 to interview with Bob Anderson, who'd founded *Runner's World*. I had written about the magazine's national launch in *Impact*, the trade magazine I edited, but had not met Bob in person before. He had asked me if I was overweight before confirming my trip: We had already established that I wasn't a runner; he explained that he couldn't have someone out of shape representing a magazine about fitness, which made sense to me. (The argument that an executive should represent the magazine's audience has been used repeatedly to keep women from the top posts at sports and male special-interest magazines. I am unaware of it ever keeping men from leading women's magazines.)

Bob's frugality matched my own: I took a flight over a Saturday night and stayed with my friend Amy in San Francisco, my only expense on the ground being a compact rental car. I had never seen runners en masse at that point, and was dumbfounded when I met Bob at a "fun run" at Canada College in Los Altos that Sunday. Hundreds of people had gathered in what looked to me like their underwear.

Bob was wiry and intense, just six years older than my twenty-three years and a few inches taller than my five feet three. He was passionate—almost messianic—about running, vehement in his distaste for smokers and the out-of-shape (I had not yet met his chubby wife), and convincing when he declared that he would build World Publications— also the home of *Bike World, Soccer World,* etc.—into a publishing enterprise as grandiose as its name.

After the run, we spent the day talking about the magazine's prospects and what I would do as newsstand manager: go to lots of newsstand industry functions, something I knew how to do well from my year at *Impact,* and try to convince wholesalers to properly care for our distribution. I probably won the job when I moved some copies of the magazine to the front display in Mac's Cigar Store in Palo Alto; company founders warm to the sight of someone else showing concern about their baby. After six hours of driving around looking at newsstands, I was beginning to be able to visualize myself living in California.

You would think that I had learned to restrict my business meetings with men to public places.

You would be wrong.

Although I was slightly nervous being alone with Bob when not in public, the earlier episode had been frightening because I was physically overpowered; since Bob and I probably weighed about the same, I felt safe. It turns out that power doesn't have to be physical.

Rather than continue talking in the car, we drove back to Bob's house in Los Altos: It was large and, I am sure, expensive, but once you were inside you couldn't tell you were in California; it could be Nouveau Riche, USA, Anywhere. We had already stopped by earlier in the day, when Bob had to shower and change after the fun run so that we could go out to brunch; his wife and children were back in Kansas for a visit. The grandfather clock's ticking echoed in the empty living room.

"Robin, this has been a great day. I really think this is going to work out." I expressed my excitement about the job and my conviction that I could handle its challenges. Bob added, "It would be good if we could go on talking; do you have dinner plans?"

"None that I can't change. I came to San Francisco to interview with you for this job, so that is more important."

"We had such a big brunch, how about if I just throw together a salad?" I was actually starving, as Bob's disdain for overweight people had made me careful to pick at my brunch of fruit salad and yogurt. I sat at the butcher-block counter in the large Los Altos kitchen as Bob made a salad. Iceberg lettuce; mealy tomatoes; and scentless, soft-crusted, imitation French bread. I listened to all his ideas for using *Runner's World*'s success to further expand his publishing empire. Mail-order sporting goods and book publishing were areas of immediate interest, and he was about to hire someone from the book publishing world whose name would surely be known to me. He talked as quickly as he chopped. The knife's thuds on the cutting board punctuated his rapid-fire sentences.

My mind wandered. Bob was the typical entrepreneur, full of ideas, liked to hear himself talk. The amount of time he was spending with me was flattering: clearly, filling the newsstand manager position was important. I knew enough of the industry jargon to feel as though I could carry my side of the conversation, and impress him with my name dropping. I would need to call one of my friends who actually worked in newsstand sales to find out what to do on my first day, if there was going to be one. I felt like the job was going to be mine. But after five hours of listening, I was more interested in planning my move: Where would I live? Would I need to buy a car? How would my parents react?

After the salad Bob made weak decaf and we sat on the velour couch in the family room. There was no sign of the children who lived there; not a toy or a crayon drawing. Outside on the deck, the wind chimes sounded as the evening Bay Area breeze came over the hills. "I want you to meet Doug Latimer, the general manager, in the morning. He can answer any of your questions about the company's finances." I nodded agreement. What time? "We start early; Doug's always in by eight; how about then?" This was going to be different from New York, where no one rolled in before nine and most editors start at ten.

"Robin, you should just stay here tonight. Save you the trouble of driving back to San Francisco, you can get an early start meeting Doug." He moved his hand to my knee.

"I'm not dressed for an office meeting."

"California is casual." The hand hasn't moved.

Perhaps I am losing my mind. His hand is on my knee and

he is proposing I spend the night in his home, with his wife and two kids visiting family in Kansas. Yet his manner is professional. I haven't noticed any sexual tension or chemistry during the entire day. This must be a test. Yes, that's it. We'd spent so much time talking about how I, a twenty-three-year-old, could fend off the lecherous men in the newsstand industry and still be effective in convincing them to display and sell Runner's World. *Now Bob is testing me to see if I could charmingly fend off a pass from a prospective boss and still get the job. That must be it.*

"That makes sense, but I really need to be at my best when meeting Doug and other employees. The impression I make on them is important."

"No, Robin, actually the only opinion that matters is mine, and I think it would work better if you stayed here. San Francisco is almost an hour away, you'll be fresher for the meetings if you stay." His beady dark eyes are fastened on mine, but there is nothing flirtatious in his tone. I still can't figure him out.

"Thanks, Bob, I appreciate it, but driving to the city is no big deal. I'll have to get used to it if I move here like we're talking about! In fact, I think I'll leave now, if that's okay with you. Can you give me directions to the office for tomorrow?"

Thank God, he has to move his hand to write down the directions. I stand up slowly, forcing myself not to leap to my feet and run to the door. Bob never made another inappropriate gesture toward me. I got the job. And, Dear Reader, I took it.

There are plenty of opportunities to get outraged as a feminist or as a woman; do not let that outrage keep you from a job or an assignment when you would be doing more for yourself—and, arguably, for women generally—by getting the job or assignment. (See the Baring It section "Clueless" and note that the women telling these stories did not let even the most outrageous behavior throw them for long.) Don't compromise your values to advance. But nor should you carry a chip on your shoulder. It will slow you down.

Once I was out of Bob's house driving back to San Francisco, I put the incident behind me. I wish I could tell you that I did a carefully reasoned analysis of the pros and cons of going to work for this man, but I didn't. I wanted the job. To this day, I don't know if Bob was making a pass or testing me. The more important fact is, I didn't sleep with him, and I got the job anyway.

Give men the benefit of the doubt. They need it, and sometimes you need them.

NAKED TRUTH #5

Viva la difference. When being female is an advantage, use it.

When I pulled off the most important meeting of my career, gender was a key factor.

I'd been in discussions with Time Inc. about whether they would fund the launch of *Parenting*, the magazine I wanted to start from scratch. I was out of money—and other funding options. Executive vice president Chris Meigher at Time Inc. was the decision maker, and he was famous for not taking risky positions. *Parenting* was riskier than the usual start-up: It would be based in San Francisco and led by someone unknown to Time Inc. (me) whose résumé wouldn't have gotten her a publisher's post at any magazine in the Time empire. What's more, *Parenting* would be Time's first women's magazine. There had not yet been a female publisher at a Time Inc. magazine. Chris decided we would need two more approvals to do the deal: Both Kelso Sutton, the CEO, and Henry Grunwald, the editor-in-chief of all Time Inc. magazines, had to bless the partnership.

The "church and state" sides of Time Inc. in 1986 were separate but shared a mutual distrust and intransigence about any changes that might shift the power balance. That did not augur well for Henry Grunwald, a man nearing retirement, to change the decades-old traditions of the leading publishing company in the world. He had every reason to say "no" to *Parenting*; it was my job to give him a reason to say "yes."

Chris Meigher and three other top executives joined us in Henry Grunwald's thirty-fourth-floor corner office. The views were sweeping, and we sat on gray couches under the bright winter sun. The office wasn't lavish other than in its size and a profusion of palm trees, which, coupled with the heat of the sun through the glass, added to a "jungle" feeling. One man lit a cigar. We were soon all perspiring from the heat, but I was conscious of being the only woman in an executive suite—for the first time in my career—and was determined not to be the one to get up and draw the curtains like some hotel's housekeeper. Finally, someone else moved to close them, to my immeasurable relief.

After walking Henry through my ideas about why the magazine would make Time Inc. proud, he asked me in his deep Austrian accent how I proposed to work with the editor, and specifically, what I would do if the editor and I did not see eye to eye. I responded, "I would explain where I think he is going wrong, and use my understanding of the readers' responses to back up my position. I trust my instincts, but I also listen to the audience." Henry asked, "And what if you and the editor still don't agree?" I replied, "Depending on the issue, if it was trivial I'd let it go, if it were important I would insist."

"What if it's important and if you still don't agree?"

"I'd fire the editor."

My words were direct, but my demeanor toward Henry was deferential—friendly and open, without challenging his authority, but without giving mine up. I sat on the edge of my couch, catty-cornered to him in his chair, facing him and making clear that his opinion was the reason I was now there. Although my words were saying that I would assert my authority over anyone else's in the areas of Henry's domain, my demeanor was conveying that I would listen to him.

Henry's mild smiles seemed to signal satisfaction with my responses, and they soon ushered in Owen Edwards (the editor I'd chosen); the meeting became much less direct until Kelso turned to Chris and asked him, "So, Chris, do you want to do this or not?" I forget the words Chris used (I think it was a sports analogy), but I couldn't understand if he was saying yes or no. Later Don Spurdle, vice president of magazine development, told me that I had really won over Henry, perhaps because I reminded Henry of his daughter, Lisa. I didn't know what a compliment that was until I read one of Lisa's novels a year later. If Henry felt fatherly toward me, and that made him amenable to an unprecedented power structure, I have no qualms about being daughterly.

It was unprecedented for Time Inc. to do a joint venture start-up—they ceded a lot of power to me—and a businessperson with editorial control was also unique.

The lesson here is that when you have to take a strong position with someone whose approval you need, you can take advantage of men's responses to you as a woman. Whether it's a fatherly reaction as in this example, or a sexually charged one, those dynamics can help. They soften the edges of your viewpoint, and makes compromising with you—even giving in to you—more palatable to your opponent.

Truth be told, I think the fact that I am five feet three has been a large advantage in dealing with short men (Henry and Chris both being in this category). Short men tend to want to keep others in their places, and are more comfortable when they can dominate physically. Of course there are exceptions: Probably my favorite boss of all time, Mel Ziegler, isn't tall, but it didn't even occur to me that one might characterize him as short until I imagined him reading this manuscript. And my least favorite boss, Jim Nelson, isn't small physically. At least, not in any visible way.

NAKED TRUTH #6

**Women are mortified by evidence of their own frailties. Don't be.
No one else notices nearly as much as you do.
Memories are short, and besides,
most men are shameless about their own failings.**

Are women CEOs more likely to be single or divorced than male CEOs? I've seen numbers that support and disprove the idea. However, women execs are acutely aware of the perception, which made me feel embarrassed about my need for a divorce early in *Parenting's* life. (Of course, that embarrassment paled compared to how I felt when my then-husband had tantrums at business functions.)

My 1988 divorce was particularly complicated, as well as visible, because under community property law in California my husband was entitled to half my interest in *Parenting*. The divorce would surely affect Time Inc.—they could even be sued. I was chagrined that Time's partnership with a woman would drag it into a divorce—this seemed a setback not just to me, but also to women.

Women's failure to promote themselves is one reason why men advance further, according to a recent *Wall Street Journal* article quoting Terri Dial, former vice chair of Wells Fargo: "Good girls don't advertise; only prostitutes advertise. We feel dirty promoting ourselves." So rather than give in to the embarrassment I felt over my very public divorce, I continued to be (in my best friend's loving words) "a whore who loves the spotlight."

My divorce undoubtedly brought more, unwelcome, attention because I am female. But in most instances, I have benefited from a higher profile than I am otherwise entitled to. Most dramatic was in the spring of 1990, after I had sold my interest in the magazine and was in New York. Deirdre Carmody of the *New York Times* contacted Time Inc. PR about interviewing me for a profile for the Business section; the section was being redesigned and would feature a big profile on the front page. They were eager to kick it off with a woman.

Your comfort, or discomfort, with the spotlight probably dates from childhood. (My daughter wants to be a "diva," so I probably am behaving similarly to my parents in this respect.) Whatever your inner feelings about attention and publicity, it comes with the territory, and if you shrink from it your career will be limited. Find your own style and go with it; audiences and reporters respond to truth, not artifice.

THE DATING BUSINESS

I would be the last person in the world to suggest that I know anything worth sharing about relationships. (My ex-husbands are guffawing right about now.) Here's one thing I know: Business romances affect men and women differently. More accurately: They affect women. Men are oblivious.

I have formed a few rules at the intersection between business and pleasure that have stood me well:

1. Do not date anyone who works in the same place or lives in the same apartment building. (I made this rule after breaking it once, with disastrous consequences.) Other divisions of the company are fine as long as you won't run into each other regularly if the relationship ends.
2. People change jobs, so an old relationship can come back to haunt. Try for a good ending.
3. Never sleep with anyone to get a job; that doesn't work. On the other hand, if you've slept with someone for the right reasons and later he can help your career, that's great.
4. Most rumors about intraoffice affairs are true.
5. Try to be discreet.
6. What seems like a good idea at 2 A.M. on the beach in Bermuda after several mai tais, probably isn't.

CLOTHING OPTIONAL

My struggle with fashion began as soon as I started my career. I wrote in my diary, at 23, "I have never had the inclination to be chic. I skip the parts of magazines where you learn to change your hairstyle; mine is still a sixties long-and-straight mop. I still feel out of place with my city friends in their Guccis, Anne Kleins, Halstons, and Diane von Furstenbergs. I'm still the slightly funky country cousin to them."

Clothing affects us as women: when we feel well dressed, we feel more confident. That's simplistic, but another way we are different from men. When Bob Anderson put his hand on my knee, my casual culottes outfit made me feel vulnerable; when Henry Grunwald and I went nose to nose, my elegant Italian suit was not Time Inc. preppy but formidable, just the way I wanted to feel.

It's taken decades for me to be less tortured by clothing. Finally I have realized what styles a five-feet-three-inch woman can wear (the fitter at the wedding shop where I got my gown remarked in full Brooklynese, "You need to wear a wedding dress; that dress would wear you"). But my decades of wrestling with fashion demons, not to mention friends with better taste, left me with a few rules:

1. **Do what feels good.** I only buy what makes me feel self-confident. I missed the power dressing of the eighties—not one blouse with a bow, thank you—because I hated it. I ignored this rule literally at my peril, and continued to wear high heels long after my left foot started hurting. During *Parenting*'s first summer, I wore sneakers and carried proper shoes in my briefcase for meetings, until I could spare three weeks in the busiest time of my life for foot surgery and recovery.

2. **Money isn't everything.** Spend more on fewer items. They will last longer, and people don't really remember what you wore last week.

3. **Pay attention I.** My mother really believed that women friends wouldn't give good fashion advice because they were competitive about attractiveness. I completely disagree, and have figured out which of my friends has good taste. At crucial moments, I listen to Carol. Currently, she is the group publisher for *Elle* magazine.

4. **Pay attention II.** What is the company's culture? While still following Rule #1, I tried to at least approach the style, or lack of it, of the company I was keeping. My lack of skills at accessorizing, for one thing, kept me from ever being slavish about this.

5. **Sexy Is OK.** (We're not talking Britney Spears here.) There have been times in my career when I dressed like a nun because I was afraid of bringing my sexuality into the workplace. At other times (like after losing pregnancy weight) dressing somewhat body consciously made me feel good, so I did it. And still do.

6. **Wear a pantsuit on the IPO road show.** Since IPOs are making a comeback, and perhaps you (and I) will be lucky enough to do one, I pass on this gem: A friend who took her company public in the nineties points out that you will be crawling across long benches in the limo, and should give up on wearing a skirt.

7. **Find a good tailor.** If you are like me and adore a fashion bargain, having the expert help to make it fit right is important and ultimately economical. This will not help when you get a "bargain" that is on sale because of its dreadful color.

8. **Take a cue from your female boss.** I didn't hire a prospective saleswoman because she wore a revealing shirt to the interview. If you are lucky enough to have a woman for a boss, you want her to feel you are a kindred spirit, not someone with completely different values.

9. **Don't check it.** Learn to travel light. I haven't, and I've paid dearly when luggage has been lost, or made impatient traveling companions wait with me in baggage claim areas. If

you're hopeless, at least carry on one business outfit and toiletries to avoid the first problem; it won't save you from the road-warrior travel-light competition, though.

10. **Don't sweat it.** I have made huge fashion errors; on a typical day I never look totally put together (even if the outfit is right, the purse or shoes are wrong, and the nails are never manicured), and have still done OK.

CLUELESS

While things have gotten somewhat easier for women in the workplace, they suffer more for lesser slights. The women I interviewed for this book have had some amazing experiences of sexism at work, immortalized here. Yet they shook it off like golden retrievers emerging from a dip, and moved on to the next challenge. And lest we be too smug that things have changed: Several of these experiences were in the nineties.

Ruth Owades had moved to St. Louis with her new husband, Joe, having landed a job at CBS Radio, then the pinnacle of the field. She had finally broken into on-air work, her dream, when her husband was offered a new job in Boston. He insisted that she remain in St. Louis to pursue her dream, but somehow her boss heard about Joe's job and "closed the door on me. I couldn't get on air any more. He just couldn't believe that I wasn't going to move."

Carol Smith was the first woman in advertising sales at the *Wall Street Journal,* launching her career in media. "When you'd go out to lunch you would get a cash advance from someone in a window. You'd write 'lunch with client' and they would give you fifty dollars. They wouldn't give me the cash; they said a woman shouldn't be carrying that much cash. I don't know if they were afraid I'd get mugged or go to Saks with the money." She demanded, and got, a corporate credit card.

Dianne Snedaker, former president of Ketchum Advertising and now chief marketing officer for First Republic Bank, still bristles at the memory of an interview for one of her first jobs after grad school. "I was interviewing for an account manager position on a douche account that the agency was in jeopardy of losing. I questioned the validity of their research, which consisted of men asking women why they douched. They turned me down and said I just wasn't right strategically for the position. I just lost it—which you should never do—and said, 'I've been interviewing for several months, and I can accept being told I am not right for some accounts. But there is no way you can tell me I couldn't handle a junior account position on a douche account.' There was a job offer from them waiting by the time I got home." She didn't take it.

You have to pick your battles. Leslie Jacobs was the youngest insurance agent to get a chartered property and casualty underwriters certification, and a rare woman in the field. She became active in the local CPCU Society chapter. "I worked my butt off," she says. "I was fully expecting to be made chapter chair. The nominating committee chose a guy who hadn't even attended meetings that year. I called every member I knew and asked them to come to the [next] meeting. I challenged the committee from the floor, and I won. I was the first female president of a local chapter. I took the name of every guy on that nominating committee and told my agents that when we were competing against them, we were going to take their business, I didn't care if we did it net of commissions."

Hilary Schneider, CEO of Knight Ridder Digital, remembers the go-go eighties. "This would never happen today, but in the old days Drexel held a famous High Yield Bond Conference every year. Space was really limited and I wouldn't have been invited because of my rank. But I was invited because they needed dance partners for clients, and I was told I had to wear a dress or skirt, no pants." She wanted the business exposure if not that of her legs, and attended happily.

Barbara Shattuck was in her twenties when she started in investment banking. "I was at Goldman Sachs, trying to get a financing done in the state of Mississippi that needed legislative approval, and the legislature only met once every two years," she says. "I was junior, so they would send me down there to try to convince the state legislators. I was sent to the local Holiday Inn to just stay and try to get meetings. Finally, they decided to do the bond financing and interviewed a bunch of firms. Six of us from Goldman went. I was the only woman and was scheduled to speak last. During the presentation a partner sent me a note saying, 'we are taking too much time; we'll just skip your part.' So we finished, and a state senator who happened to be blind said, 'Miss Shattuck, I know you are there even though I can't see you. You've been talking to me for months; why aren't you saying anything now?' I learned never to be the last one scheduled to speak." And I daresay the men learned something too, to their own detriment, about excluding women.

Jan Brandt, former president of marketing and vice chair of AOL, recalls, "At a senior executive meeting a man and a woman from another company were making a presentation to sell something to us. He was clearly deferential to her. She led the presentation. My colleague leaned over toward the end of the presentation and whispered, 'It wasn't until halfway through the meeting that I realized she is his boss. I have such a tough time realizing that the woman can be the boss.' I probably had three hundred people working for me at that point."

Are male colleagues still this clueless?
Please share your stories at *www.nakedintheboardroom.com*.

TWO

Burn
Your Career Plan

I DON'T KNOW WHEN COLLEGES STARTED TEACHING STU-dents to plan their careers. Most of the young people I meet now, fresh out of college or graduate school, earnestly believe that they need a plan for their progression through jobs and life. They have everything mapped out. For each company they interview with, they know how to analyze its growth prospects (and theirs within the company) and have plotted out the trajectory of their careers based on their prospective initial jobs.

This is not such a good thing.

The fun, self-discovery, and serendipity of launching a career have been taken out of the process. People taking a first job are self-protective and cautious, though there is little at risk. Sure, it may take months to find a job and start making payments on school loans. But since the job won't pay much anyway, the opportunity cost isn't as big as it feels. Individuals who believe they will fail if the first, or second, or tenth job they take doesn't make logical sense in the fleshing-out of their résumés are doomed from the get-go. They think they need to know whether their future path is in business development or marketing or finance by the time they are twenty-eight. They worry about how long—or short—a stay with a company will look to the next employer.

As an employer, I find these prospective employees un-appealing. They can, and do, talk endlessly about their career plans. But they don't have a lot to say about what they can do *for the company*. They rarely show an authentic interest in the company or its products. I'm not talking about a lifelong dream of working for a particular company (few can say at twenty-five that they've always really wanted to work at *Aeronautical Systems* magazine), but even a positive word about a company's vibe, or a passing admiration for a specific product or corporate policy, is a good place to start.

NAKED TRUTH #7

Relax and enjoy your early career. Now's the time to put in longer hours and extra effort, before family obligations and awareness of life's brief time horizon set in.

When I graduated from college few of my peers even knew what a résumé looked like. We weren't designing Careers; we were simply looking to get started. So take a flier. Learn what companies are like, and what characteristics inspire you—and which drive you crazy. Figure out what kind of boss brings out the best in you. The great thing about early jobs is how easy it is to move on: You're not making much money, so you can afford to risk a change. If you don't find work that interests you—or boring work in a good company where you can make a mark—you have little to lose by moving on.

Moreover, these early jobs provide excellent training at the simple process of working within an organization. In school, the assumption is that all participants are respected and you will continue to progress if you study hard and don't repeatedly screw up badly. In the corporate world, you have to earn the right to progress—and sometimes "earning it" has nothing to do with hard work. After that rude awakening, you will see that for the first time, you are truly on your own. That can be exhilarating when things go well; when they don't, you need to develop coping mechanisms.

Working, you will acquire skills that are crucial even if you can't list them on a résumé. If you are disorderly, like me, you learn tricks to keep your tasks prioritized. You see whether the preferred communication is email, voicemail, or hallway meeting. You learn that friends in other departments with less glamorous titles may be having more fun and making more money.

You learn truths such as that excelling at performing boring tasks is just as big an accomplishment as achieving more creative or innovative goals. It's also probably more appreciated by your employer—not to mention more common. Recent college graduates often expect their work to be intellectually stimulating from day one. The truth is, you're at the bottom of the pecking order and have to pay some dues. I might have had an Ivy League degree, but I never found it demeaning to get coffee for my boss, as long as the company was paying me. That attitude is old-fashioned now, I know, but it applies to the current list of petty tasks that admins (formerly assistants, formerly secretaries) need to do.

If I had ever had a plan, business would not have been part of it. A career in business never occurred to me while growing up. (Although some colleagues would probably think it portentous that my sixth-grade teacher cast me as Lady Macbeth without having me read for the part, saying I was the only possible choice.) I had chosen my college, the Industrial and Labor Relations School at Cornell, because it was an affordable (state division) ticket to a law degree and, not coincidentally, an easy drive to my boyfriend's college. If I had thought about a career in labor relations, which I didn't, it would have been—reflexively—on the union side; management would have been anathema. As my classmates rabidly competed in planning their legal careers (90 percent of the school's 1975 graduates chose that path), I assumed I would as well. I just wasn't quite ready, yet.

I'd held jobs throughout my junior and senior years at Cornell. Others might have considered the jobs boring: One semester I typed (it had to be letter perfect) the text of *Insects, Science, and Society* in the entomology department. The typing was tedious, but I liked the women in the office, the grad student I briefly dated did a great job ridding our apartment of cockroaches, and I loved seeing my name in the acknowledgments. These early jobs helped me develop an important skill: finding satisfaction in achievements I could measure myself, and not to rely on praise from my boss.

Since most bosses are woefully bad at praising your achievements, you will be a much happier employee if you judge yourself—rigorously, but pausing to note the successes. (Politely communicate them to your boss instead of silently waiting for someone to notice. Some would call this self-promotion a negative trait, but it is a necessary skill and one that women are much worse at than men, so start learning early.)

Another semester I cataloged memorabilia of the United Transportation Union in my school's library. Mostly this involved describing items like the embosser a conductor used to punch tickets, but one discovery remains with me. As I studied a photograph taken at a train station, I was thrilled to realize that the man in the stovepipe hat was Abraham Lincoln. I didn't need my boss to praise me for finding a rare Mathew Brady photograph.

NAKED TRUTH #8

Learn to be your own evaluator, and find the benchmarks to know how you're doing, even when your boss won't tell you.

Much of what I enjoyed about these rather rote jobs was the sense of belonging with my coworkers. I had never been a popular kid. In junior high and high school I was never part of the in crowd: too studious to be a real hippie, yet too interested in boys and rock 'n' roll to be a nerd. In working, I found a ready-made clique that automatically included me. And instead of being filled with people just like myself, like my high school friends (smart, semirebellious Jewish girls), these cliques introduced me to people from different backgrounds.

I even enjoyed my waitress jobs; one, at a bar in Collegetown, required me to wear a short skirt and low-cut top, but I liked the early-morning diner breakfasts we all went to after closing the bar. And in my last semester, with a very light schedule, I worked full-time at Hal's Deli, and felt richer than I had ever been (or would be), coming home greasy but with my pockets stuffed with more tips than I could spend. Friends who know me as a klutz and someone who doesn't like to take orders are often surprised at how much I liked being a waitress: The instant report card appealed to me.

I didn't realize it at the time, of course, but after years of coaching young women at the beginning of their careers, I know that a great result of early, menial jobs was that I thrived without feedback from my supervisors. Today's young professionals are hungry for feedback and feel entitled to it. Think about it: If progression up the career ladder is tied to achievement, the law of averages means that your bosses in your early jobs will be the least skilled ones you will encounter. You will need to measure your own performance and create your own report card. This is a skill worth developing, because if your boss later in your career is like I am, she will ask you to do a self-evaluation rather than give you one out of the blue. (It's less work for her.) So early on, learn to figure out the measures of success, and hold yourself to them.

I write a note to myself at the beginning of a job, or a new project. I set a timeline for when success can be measured, and what it will look like. I then put the note into my calendar (this is all electronic now, but I used to do it on scraps of paper; whatever works for you) and revisit it. If the outcome wasn't the success I had listed, I ask why: Did it not succeed? Or did success look different? Was the roadblock external and truly insurmountable, or was the shortcoming mine? If successful, what would I have done even better?

Become your own toughest critic, but don't share the self-criticism.

Showing honest emotion usually helps you in the workplace.

A job I stumbled into during the summer between high school and college ultimately changed my life. Jobs were not plentiful in 1971, so I signed up with Career Blazers, a temporary employment agency. I was thrilled when they told me they had a weeklong assignment for me on Wall Street; I could commute on the Long Island Railroad with my father. At the end of the first day of incredibly boring work in a typing pool at Paine Webber, I was told by the woman who supervised the clerks, "You did a really good job. If we need a typist again I'll ask Career Blazers for you." I stammered, "But they told me the job was for a week." She said no, it was just for the day. Tears streaming down my cheeks, I told her that I had bought my train ticket for the week—the day's pay wouldn't even cover that. I didn't want to burst into tears, but it caused my supervisor to see me as a person instead of a faceless temp. She immediately got on the phone to Career Blazers and told them that if they ever wanted to work for Paine Webber Jackson & Curtis again, they would find a job for me for the rest of the week.

I spent Tuesday at Career Blazers's midtown office, stuffing envelopes and doing other busywork. They got a call for a prospective job, and told me that I should go to the office near Times Square, but not to worry if I didn't like it, to just come back to Career Blazers and they would find me something else for the remainder of the week. Apparently they had not had a lot of success placing temps at *Penthouse* magazine.

I'm not recommending tears in the workplace. Although

if you are like me and well up at an American Express commercial, the effort of holding back tears may not be worth it: Often I am more distracted by trying *not* to cry than I would be if a few wet ones escaped. Years later, as a new (and nursing) mother, I cried copiously (and regrettably) when my boss told me I'd lost his confidence. To keep my job, he explained, I would need to regain the confidence of *his* boss, Don Logan, the CEO of Time Inc.

When you are headed into an all-important meeting that has the potential to reduce you to tears, preparation is essential. I knew the areas that pushed my buttons, and steered clear of them: feeling betrayed by my boss; indignation over the different standards being applied to me and to male colleagues. Don was looking forward, so I needed to. Believe me, not a tear came close to the surface when I talked with Don. Yet I am pretty much incapable of a poker face, and don't want one. I told Don, "I know I overlooked the signs of problems with the advertising staff. They'd been trained not to bring problems to management, and I was used to the *Parenting* environment, where everyone was free to surface problems. I didn't dig deep enough, but it will never happen again. I am disappointed in myself, but I have learned from it." I took ownership of the problem, and let Don know how I felt and what I would do to recover the situation. Honest emotion, not tears, if you can help it.

NAKED TRUTH #10

Opportunity is more likely to fall into your lap if you are at a fast-moving company. Choose a growing, or at least a changing, business over a prestigious one.

There is luck involved in career advances, but you can improve your odds. If you are hung up on prestige or emotional connection to a product, you may choose jobs at stagnant companies. In my industry, going to work for *Penthouse* in 1971 was slightly embarrassing; an equivalent job at the *New Yorker* would have been prestigious (and, for me, deadly). At *Penthouse* there was more work than people to do it; at the *New Yorker*, the senior people would keep all the interesting stuff to themselves.

I had vaguely heard of *Penthouse*, which had just come to the United States two years earlier, and thought it was like *Playboy*. As I walked through Times Square on my first day I wondered whether the offices would be like the engineering firm where my father worked—the only other office I'd visited. It was the height of the sexual revolution, and my highest aspiration was to have a job for the summer; I assumed that most of the people who worked at *Penthouse* had to sleep with someone to get their jobs. When I saw the receptionist in gold lamé hot pants, my fantasies about working there became even more lurid. One of the first items of office decor that caught my eye was a poster in the cubicle of a female editor. A photograph of a woman from the waist down, clad in a pair of partially unzipped tight jeans, it read "Fit in or fuck off."

This was not my father's office.

While I was waiting in the secretarial bullpen, listening to the radio softly playing "Maggie May" (a song that needs to be blasted), a heavy, balding, middle-aged man with a red face came puffing into the room. "I need a secretary!" Joe Coleman, the advertising director, panted. "What about you, are you a secretary?" I said, "I'm just a temp." "How would you like to be permanent?" I said I'm going to school in

September. "Okay, how would you like to be permanent to September?" I was hired—before I had typed a word.

I got the job just by being in the right place at the right time. The reason they kept me—and kept offering me summer and Christmas vacation jobs throughout college—is that I worked as hard as I could, never complained when asked to do something that appeared trivial, and knew I didn't know anything but was smart enough to figure almost everything out. Unlike prestigious magazines where the other secretaries would also have been well-educated, smart, and ambitious, I had little competition from the women who saw no future beyond typing.

NAKED TRUTH #11

If you have a sense of humor, keep it handy.

Knowing when to stick up for yourself can make the difference between being a whiner and a winner. I haven't been perfect at drawing that line, but one reason I've won is that when I speak out, I do it with some humor. One day I typed a memo for one of the women execs at *Penthouse*. She came into the typists' area waving it at me. "Who's the fucking moron who typed this?"

"I typed it."

"I thought you were the college kid. Who the fuck spells Steel with an e at the end?" snarled Dawn Steel, later legendary as the first female president of a major movie studio and a notoriously tough boss.

"My boyfriend and his whole family. They changed it

differently at Ellis Island." Dawn and I got along fine after that.

Humor will serve you well as you grow in business stature. As the thirty-eight-year-old new CEO of Sunset, my management team included a man over sixty who hugged me during a group meeting, wordlessly saying, "Isn't she cute." I waited until I could see him privately to explain why this was not suitable. He was horror-struck that I thought he was harassing me sexually. I explained, somewhat wryly, that it wasn't sexual harassment, just not the way to treat the boss, and he later told me that my humor and gentleness with the rebuke was the best handling of a tricky personal situation that he'd seen in his career. (And he gracefully retired when I wanted him to.)

NAKED TRUTH #12

Before worrying overly about your job's lack of challenge—and certainly before complaining about it—concentrate on delivering.

If there is one thing I look for from a beginning employee, it's evidence of a work ethic. Willingness to do any task without complaint is also appreciated. This is good news, though: A little bit of work ethic goes a long way today. It will set you apart from the crowd.

Penthouse was growing rapidly in those years. During my monthlong winter breaks and summers, I worked in various departments: as a receptionist who kept my copy of *Sisterhood Is Powerful* on the desk; in the circulation department where I entered sell-through numbers by hand into a large green ledger, recording the results of newsstand wholesalers in towns I'd never heard of before; in the editorial department transcribing *Penthouse*'s famous letters, especially the ones directed at Xaviera Hollander, the happy hooker. The last was really my only salacious job at *Penthouse*; I was glad to wear headphones when transcribing the tapes so that no one knew what I was listening to. (And it has allowed me to answer the first question asked by every man who learns about my employment history: No, we didn't write the letters; we just edited them for grammar and clarity. For some reason, most of the letters dealt with fantasies of, or actual, sex with amputees. I couldn't make the math work: where were all the amputees with whom these guys were cavorting? I hadn't noticed enough amputees to people these letters, although perhaps they just didn't walk around. The letter that remains in my memory—perhaps because of my 100 word-per-minute skills—was from the man who put his penis where the roller of his Smith Corona typewriter normally resided. I still can't figure out how he could reach the keys.)

Perhaps your early career jobs weren't as titillating as that one. Yet over the years, in addition to the obvious benefit of being launched in my publishing career, lessons from my earliest jobs still stick with me: Driving through a new area of the country I will see a highway sign with a town name that I know from those circulation ledger sheets; my kids will be amazed because, despite my usual clumsiness, my waitress experience allows me to carry multiple dinner plates simultaneously; or I'll be hiring an assistant and intuitively know which candidate resembles which type of assistant with whom I toiled before the term "admin" was invented. Learning happens in every job, but you have to pay attention.

Several months after graduating from college, I abruptly changed my plan of working for a year at *Penthouse* before proceeding to law school. Instead of a temporary respite from my education, work became a career. Thus began a career-long habit of seeing opportunity and jumping. That year I began working in the public relations department. Despite my feminism, I found it easy to sell *Penthouse*. But *Penthouse's* sister magazine, *Viva*, was a hard magazine to promote. Allegedly for women, it featured photos of reclining men with limp, albeit huge, penises—erections apparently verboten. I couldn't imagine any women I knew reading the magazine, and the magazine's numbers bore me out: In those pre–gay rights days, most of the purchasers of the magazine were men. (This did not help in attracting cosmetics advertisers.) After consultation with my boss I wrote a memo to *Penthouse* owners Bob Guccione and Kathy Keeton that in another company would have gotten me fired. The gist of the memo was that I couldn't sell *Viva*. It made no sense as a magazine: The only surprise was that *Penthouse's* distribution prowess managed to sell three hundred thousand copies of *Viva* a month. Some of the articles were hard-edged feminism; some were *Penthouse*-like slutty; some were incomprehensible. The photos were not for women and not erotic.

I mitigated the risk of going to the top of the company by keeping my immediate boss informed about my intentions. My viewpoint turned out to coincide with her aspirations. Bob and Kathy fired the editorial staff of *Viva* and banished male nudes. My boss, Alma Moore, was made editorial director. Because I was willing to speak my mind I became an associate editor, a job for which I had no qualifications but little competition.

You may be surprised at top management's obliviousness to the reasons for a project's struggles or imminent failure. What is clear to the people working directly on a failure is sometimes foggy to those at the top. Yet most employees mutter among themselves, get demoralized, and end up out of a job when the inevitable failure happens. If you have a better idea, voice it, respectfully, keeping your direct boss in the loop, but to the people who matter—not to your peers. If top management doesn't welcome feedback on a struggling project, you probably don't want to work there anyway.

NAKED TRUTH #14

If you're not over your head with a new job, you haven't moved far enough.

I was clueless as to what an associate editor did. The art department would inform me that captions had to be exactly equal in length (for graphic balance) and I didn't know enough to say that that was ridiculous, so I made them equal.

I compensated for lack of knowledge by working around-the-clock. This was easy: I had no social life, or money to do much, and my waist-length hair and clogs, which had worked in Ithaca, were less successful in Manhattan. I got some well-meaning help from the male editors of *Penthouse*, most of whom I had worked for. It was the first example of something that has happened over and over in my career: Because I work hard and am nice to people, they help me out. I also learned that I thrive on public recognition. It's embarrassing to admit it, but perhaps not as embarrassing as being motivated by money or competitive fervor; I like seeing my name in print.

People respond differently to the feeling of being over their heads with new responsibilities. My friend Carol panics that she will be fired, and the thought of being fired never crosses my mind (even when it's about to happen). But we are similar in that we both grasp desperately at lifelines: working around-the-clock; calling on friends and vendors for advice and assistance; and being determined to beat the odds.

I'll make a gross gender generalization: Men don't like to admit they have lost control (e.g., asking for directions), so they enter new jobs with sublime self-confidence; their powers of denial are impressive. Women measure themselves against impossible standards—the perfect résumé—so often are in new jobs feeling unprepared. Don't worry about asking for directions. Whoever gave you the opportunity for a new job wants you to succeed, not fail. Be sure you know your boss's expectations for success. Ease up on your personal benchmarking for a short time, and go into learning mode for your honeymoon period. Maybe even read a business book.

Although I was fairly well qualified for the general manager position of *Mother Jones* when I took it, the job changed on my second day there. The publisher (the boss who'd hired me) was resigning and a search for a new one would be launched; I was the only potential internal candidate. I knew perfectly well that I was not ready to be a publisher, and opted out of the search.

The publisher of *Marxist Perspectives* (circulation about 1 percent of *MoJo*'s, if I remember correctly) was chosen, and I spent the next year trying to teach him the economics of publishing. When his failure was obvious and his departure terms had been worked out, the editors launched another search. This time I said I would wait and see the caliber of the applicants. I still wasn't ready to be a publisher (I was twenty-seven), but rather than face another year of training my boss, I would throw my hat in the ring if no one more qualified was found. That's how I became the youngest publisher of a national magazine.

Four years later, I had grown bored at *Mother Jones* and wanted to earn more money. I did a careful evaluation of my skills and started to interview for better-paying publishing jobs and for direct-marketing positions outside of publishing. As I considered possibilities in the magazine publishing field, I told my friends what I believed: I would be the "perfect number two." (Not recognizing the Naked Truth above, I was comparing myself to an ideal. The problem was, I didn't know of a perfect number one.) I was beginning to realize that maybe I could play that role: I knew publishing economics inside out (running a money-losing magazine is a great teacher); I was known for my network of talented pals; and I had a rare balance of editorial and business experience.

You need to think about what you bring to a job, not what you lack. Let others worry about the holes in your résumé. For me, focusing on other candidates is the surest way to get past my self-doubt. I may not be perfect, but if I am less imperfect than other real-life candidates, I can do it.

My primary need in planning a career move was for more money. I'd been working for a nonprofit, and I had just married a man who'd declared bankruptcy the day after our hasty wedding. Any of the jobs for which I interviewed—in publishing or direct marketing—would have more than doubled my pay. For once I was less concerned with finding a job that I would love. So, of course, I ended up working for no money—going into debt—to follow my passion. I cover the launch of *Parenting* magazine in a later chapter; here I will just note that working without pay, when for the first time I had pressing financial needs, was the best career plan I've ever burned.

THE BEST BURNT PLANS OF SUCCESSFUL WOMEN

The women I interviewed for this book became presidents or CEOs. Many are company founders. All are currently in their forties or fifties, so like me they came of age in a different era from today's women who are still on the upward trajectories of their careers. At that time, it was just beginning to be assumed that smart women would go to college; to the extent they thought about careers, most of these women thought about medicine, the law, or teaching. Business didn't occur to most of us. Perhaps because their careers took such unexpected paths, they have a lot of wisdom to share about planning. Not one thought it was possible or even desirable to plan a career path while in school.

Because these women have reached pinnacles in their respective industries, younger women frequently ask their advice. Karen S. Behnke, founder and former president of Execu-Fit Health Programs, a corporate wellness provider she sold to PacificCare, put it succinctly: "Women ask me all the time, 'How can I get training for such-and-such position?' 'I'm not qualified; how can I get the qualifications for the next step?' I say, 'What makes you think you're not qualified?' Men never question their own qualifications. Forget your résumé. Whatever you need to do to shore yourself up at midnight or in the shower, do it. Get support wherever you can find it." Karen's pluckiness is understandable. Educated for a career in nursing, she started her company at twenty-five; an aerobics instructor, she financed the company with seventeen credit cards.

But you don't need to be a company founder to have the same spirit. Almost every woman used the same word: "serendipity." They expressed sadness that many women today want to plan their careers, because they feel that their biggest successes came because they were open to unexpected opportunities. Barbara Shattuck changed career plans twice. "I always had an interest in health care, I thought I would be a physician until organic chemistry in college did me in." She changed to environmental studies, planning a career in environmental design. "I had done a land-use planning study for Waterford, Connecticut, with a Ford Foundation grant. The study for Waterford happened to be about water systems. I had no money and had to work. Standard & Poor's wanted someone in public finance, as they were doing credit ratings for water and sewer systems. I didn't know anything about finance, but I was hired. It started out as a horrible job; I just thought I would do it until I got married and moved into the house with a picket fence. Then they decided to assign credit ratings to hospitals—my original interest had been in health care. It was great serendipity." Because of her finance experience, she got a job at Goldman Sachs in investment banking—"a business I didn't know existed." At thirty-two she founded her company, now called Shattuck Hammond Partners, an independent investment banking and financial advisory firm specializing in health care services and other industries.

Hilary Schneider, CEO of Knight Ridder Digital, echoes the theme: "Serendipity is so important. I wouldn't normally say it in an interview, because I like to make myself look more of a planner. But at Harvard [Business School] all I ever wanted to be was an investment banker—I blew off marketing, human behavior, other courses that could have helped me. I wanted to work for Drexel and I got a job in the Beverly Hills office. By happenstance the first deal I worked on was a newspaper acquisition. This made me the media expert in the office, so for four years I got to do those deals. I had become a VP, and suddenly Drexel went out of business. If that hadn't happened I'd probably still be in investment banking. Someone suggested I call Alice Greenthal at Times Mirror newspapers bcause she had been ahead of me at HBS, so I cold-called her. She said, 'I don't have a job for you' but agreed to have lunch. Then she hired me. I started in M and A [mergers and acquisitions] and moved to operating roles."

Ginger L. Graham, president and CEO of Amylin, a pharmaceutical company focused on diabetes and other metabolic diseases, adds, "I was born believing I would be a veterinarian. I went to pre–vet school, worked for a vet. I realized I didn't want to do it." The theme of Ginger's career was that she would take a job if it meant working for a bright person from whom she thought she could learn. Sometimes this led to unexpected turns, like her first job after graduation from Harvard Business School working on

Japanese expansion for Eli Lilly. A month after she started, the Lilly board rejected the proposal. "So I took the death title of a job— 'manager of special projects'— because it reported to the person who was expected to be the next CEO. No one else wanted this. But it put me in front of the executive committee frequently, exposed to lots of different people and areas. It ended up with my involvement in the largest-value sale of a cosmetics company at that time."

For Ruth Owades, keeping an open door was literally the way to a new life. "My first job was a job working for the Economic Development Board of the city of Los Angeles, based in New York. I was a gofer/secretary/girl Friday in a two-person office, and often there alone. Mayor [Sam] Yorty told me to keep the door open when I was alone so I could scream for help. Because the door was open, a man visiting the company in an adjacent office stopped in and I married him one-and-a-half years later." Following her husband's career moved her to Boston, where she tried to continue her early work in broadcast. "It was hard to get a job in Boston, so I got a horrible TV job in a suburb. I tried to convince my boss that we needed to cover more than murder and mayhem, and he wouldn't listen to me at all. I got into my car, pulled out a map, and said, 'Where is Harvard?' I found the law school and the business school. I chose the business school because it was only two years, law was three." Now she is not just a business school graduate, but the subject of several Harvard case studies because she successfully founded the Gardener's Eden catalog (then selling it to Williams-Sonoma) and then Calyx & Corolla (sold to an investor group).

Sometimes friends or colleagues realized the right path before these women figured it out themselves. Marion McGovern worked for Boston Consulting Group in college and planned to be a consultant. She needed an MBA for her first job, so she worked for Arthur D. Little, a consulting firm, while in business school. "David Partridge, a senior person with the firm, and I were working together and he asked me, 'What kind of business will you start?' I replied, 'I want to be a partner in a consulting firm, like you.' He said, 'No way. You'll start a business.' Ten years later, after starting my business, I was with my daughters in an airport and ran into him. When I reminded him of the conversation he looked at my kids and assumed that's what I had done instead of starting a business." Marion gently told him that in addition to being a mother she is the cofounder and president of M2, a brokerage of independent consultants.

P. K. Scheerle, RN, president and CEO of American Nursing Services, laughs and calls herself a slow learner in this regard. ("Maybe because I graduated two hundred fortieth in a class of 240—although with the top SATs.") She had left one job working for a nursing-outsourcing company because she wanted to continue to work as a nurse as well as salesperson/manager; hired by a competitor, she built the next firm until its owner lost the company due to financial mismanagement. When the new owner began their relationship by telling her "You're going to realize that running a business isn't playing house," she resigned; the company's accountant walked her to her car, told her she was the reason for the company's success, and that if she wanted to start her own business he would sign the loans and be her 50/50 partner. One successful year later he wanted to be bought out. She has owned the company, which now has 30 branches and 4,000 nurses who staff hospital ICUs, since 1985.

Anne Bakar tossed her career plan because of tragedy, not serendipity. A political philosophy major who'd worked for Ralph Nader, she had expected to go to law school, but three months at a law firm had been more than enough. She spent seven years in business, rising as an analyst at Montgomery Securities covering technology. Her father ran a small health care business with $24 million in revenue and 500 employees. He was diagnosed with cancer in 1987 and died from treatment complications several weeks later. "I had never managed more than a secretary before. If my father had asked me to join the company, the answer would have been no. We had one conversation after his diagnosis, and he commented that the business would be boring for me. But he showed that he trusted me; he made me trustee of our family's estate. I felt that what the company was doing was important. I had passion for it as well as vision." Anne took over the business, Telecare Corporation, a provider of services to people with serious psychiatric disabilities, which today has $125 million in annual revenue. "I probably would have made more money if I stayed at Montgomery. But I love what we do."

THREE

How to Listen to Your Gut

I HAVE USUALLY MADE THE BEST DECISIONS WITHOUT AGO-nizing over (or even being aware of) the fork in the road: I just did what felt right. I learned over decades in business that following the direction that gave me a peaceful stomach and unknotted shoulders led to more job satisfaction than making a list on a yellow pad of pluses and minuses.

Many factors conspire to muffle the sounds our guts are making. The biggest message-mufflers:

- **Ego.** A dead giveaway is when you spend more time thinking about others' reactions to your move than on the content of what you are moving to. If you are drawn to a new position because of its lofty title, ego can be trumping your instincts.
- **Greed.** Here's the thing about money: The more you have, the more you need. If more money's one of your top two

reasons for doing something, and you're not destitute, think again.

- **Our parents' voices.** A friend of mine was the third child, and told often that he was just not as smart as his siblings; ultimately, he was much more successful than either, but never achieved his full potential, moving to the top position at a small company and staying there long after he got bored. He got past his parents' low-confidence vote, but barely.
- **Others' expectations.** For women, the "good-girl" messages from our parents, friends, and society-at-large lead to self-consciousness and an overly developed sense of obligation.

It may be hard to trust your gut in the beginning of your career, but that's when messages can be most clear, when you have little experience to go on and little to lose. Women are so worried about being too emotional that we often try to overcompensate by being logical at the expense of listening to our hearts. Call it women's intuition, emotional intelligence, or gut instinct, but don't let your MBA or other formal training get in the way of your most important guide.

NAKED TRUTH #16

Your body may give you signs before your brain has figured out your next move. Pay attention to illnesses that may be psychosomatic, and to your general physical condition.

Negative messages are sometimes the easiest to hear. I had had a year of great success at my first "real" job after college, as a features editor of *Viva, Penthouse*'s failing sister magazine. As the magazine floundered, the owners brought in a new editor who convened his first meeting of the all-female editorial staff and told us, "It's going to be tough to be a male editor of a women's magazine. After all, I only know what it's like to fuck, not to be fucked." My advancement at *Viva* had been quick and rewarding; I loved seeing my byline on a national magazine's pages; I was making more money than I needed; and I was deeply loyal to the company. It took a dramatic scene to get the message to my gut.

That night, while I told Paula Siegel, a friend and writer for the magazine, about the meeting, my left hand shook uncontrollably, and she said, "It's time for you to quit." I then called my oldest friend, Amy Weiss, who was soon embarking on a cross-country move to San Francisco, and she urged me to come for the ride. *Penthouse* had been my employer for years, from my first job through college and my first year after graduation, but I made the decision easily.

Research is the first refuge of managers afraid of trusting their own instincts. Focus groups, mall intercepts, mailed surveys, eyeball-movement analysis: I've seen lots of techniques used when managers are afraid to go with their guts. Dianne Snedaker, whose marketing career used research many times, commented, "We did a lot of work for food companies. I would put samples outside my office. If employees weren't coming back for seconds—or if they didn't even once pick up the free taste—I didn't need to spend money to know the product would be a dud." Whether it's your appetite or that of your customers, paying attention to physical responses will lead to better decisions than the most expensive consumer research.

The most likely time to ignore messages from your gut is when following your gut means making an inconvenient or difficult decision, or delays reaching a goal.

The woman I'd thought would head advertising sales during *Parenting*'s launch called me the day before the business plan was being printed. She had taken a job at *Esquire*. My terror at printing a business plan with only my name on it was mitigated by something akin to relief: Our working relationship had been difficult as we negotiated long and hard over her proposed salary (if I had put her requested salary into the plan, no sane investor would have agreed), bonus, title, equity, etc. She made the decision not to wait for a risky launch, and I learned (not for the first or last time) to listen to my gut, which had been uncomfortable about our negotiating dynamics.

Although that episode ultimately worked out for me—I found a much better person—I should have broken off the negotiations and started a new search, rather than waiting for her to leave me in the lurch.

* * *

Why do we ignore personal chemistry when making a key hire? We get overwhelmed by the right résumé, and by how others will laud us when we tell them this highly qualified person wants to work for us. Instead, think about how you feel just before an important conversation with the prospective business partner or hire. Do you feel a need to prepare, to outline your thoughts, to anticipate their reaction? Or do you just pick up the phone, or walk into their office, and start talking? The first set of behaviors should be a red flag.

NAKED TRUTH #18

**Don't heed advice just because you're paying for it.
Experts don't know everything.**

Expert advice and other people's opinions can overwhelm your own gut instincts—especially when your gut has the flu.

I was feverish and achy when my husband, lawyer, and I met a negotiating team from Time Inc. about the *Parenting* launch at a suite in the Stanford Court Hotel. Professor William A. Sahlman of the Harvard Business School wrote a case study about the decision I faced, and thousands of business school students at Harvard and other schools around the world have now studied this case.* An excerpt follows:

*Copyright © by the President and Fellows of Harvard College. Harvard Business School Case 9-291-015

Robin Wolaner was distracted as the waiter at the Rue Lepic restaurant in downtown San Francisco, California asked what she wanted to order. Wolaner, her husband, and a legal advisor had just terminated negotiations with a team representing Time Inc. about a much needed $5 million investment in her plan to launch a new magazine called Parenting. Negotiations had reached an impasse, with both sides digging in their heels. The Time team had left the all-day negotiating session remarking that they thought a deal would be impossible, given the bargaining intransigence of the Wolaner group. They were headed to the airport to take the "red-eye" back to New York. It was March 27, 1986.

The particular negotiating impasse between the Time representatives and Wolaner concerned the terms under which Time might buy Wolaner's ownership in the magazine venture. Basically, Time wanted to have the option to purchase Wolaner's stake at a point three years from the signing of the contract for a price that would be capped, no matter how well the magazine was doing at that time or what the fair market value would be. Wolaner's advisors were adamant: there should be no cap. Time could buy Wolaner out, but the purchase price should be related to the then-current market value of the magazine.

My husband and our lawyer were outraged by Time's position. Instead of focusing on what the deal would yield us—more than $10 million in three years if things went according to plan—they were offended that Time would have the temerity to cap our upside. I didn't get it, but thought it must be the flu clogging my brain, since these two smart people were so sure of themselves.

Wolaner had acceded to her advisors during the meeting, but was now having second thoughts. If the project worked, the buyout price would still yield a substantial sum, particularly for someone who had spent the previous five years working as publisher of Mother Jones, a non-profit magazine based in San Francisco. Did it really matter if the price wasn't "fair market value"? Moreover, raising money from venture capitalists would surely entail giving up a substantial piece of the pie, even if there were no cap on the ultimate value.

I tried not to listen to my husband when making business decisions, but I was hesitant to overrule an expensive lawyer whose expertise was in early-stage deals and financings.

It wasn't easy for Wolaner to collect her thoughts, but she would have to decide quickly: if not, her dream of starting Parenting might go for naught.

I felt like my head was going to explode. My husband and our lawyer were talking about how greedy Time Inc. was and how they were trying to take advantage of us. How dare they try to cap the upside from this venture? I struggled to understand the reason for their anger. Advice from Arthur Dubow, my first investor, rang in my ears: Only losers obsess about what the other party in a negotiation gets; winners concentrate on getting what they need.

I decided before the crème brûlée arrived. Some lawyers

make deals happen and others make them fall apart. For whatever reason, this lawyer was wrong.

I said, "I don't get it. If the magazine is successful—which is the only way the cap becomes important—I would still be getting over ten million three or four years from now. And no one else is offering us *anything*. Why should we lose this deal just because you think someone else might not cap our upside?" They were briefly silent, and then agreed with me. I went home and set my alarm for 4 A.M. so I could reach Spurdle, my first Time Inc. partner, before he had to report to his boss on the collapse of our negotiations.

I followed my gut instead of the lawyers, and made a deal with Time Inc. that changed my life. I confess that a short time later, however, I ignored my gut—and paid the price.

NAKED TRUTH #19

When you know something is right and inevitable, don't put it off to protect your emotional well-being. Like tearing off a Band-Aid: Get it over with.

During our weeks of working out the details of the partnership agreement, Don Spurdle, then head of magazine development at Time, took me to dinner at a Milton Glaser–designed restaurant (that means it was beautiful and expensive, although now defunct and I've forgotten its name) on Fiftieth Street in New York City. After several drinks, he was ready to broach the subject that clearly was the reason for the dinner.

His boss, Chris Meigher, and he were uncomfortable with my husband's continuing presence at meetings and involvement in decisions at the magazine and wanted the contract to confirm that he would receive no compensation and play no formal role. Because I'd had some wine myself (a good reason not to drink at business dinners), I started crying in total despair. Under more sober circumstances, I could have kept the tears back, but I still would have been stymied. I knew that putting this into the agreement would cause a huge explosion in my shaky marriage, and I didn't know how to handle it. I told Don that I totally agreed that my husband needed to stay out of the magazine's operations, but that putting it into the agreement might derail everything. I promised that he would receive no compensation and have no title beyond "cofounder," an honorific without official powers. Some weeks after this dinner I saw the first sketches for the offices we were having built; my husband had negotiated the lease and was working with the architect I chose, and to my dismay I saw an office labeled "cofounder." After I lost the argument on this point, I had to tell this unwelcome news to Don.

There was never going to be an opportune moment for dealing with my husband's desire for a role in the business. If I had confronted the problem then, when my partner at Time brought up their concerns, it would have been better for the business, and for me.

I paid a high price for ignoring my gut and allowing my husband to continue to try to play a role at the magazine. One example of the toll it took was the ruining of what should have been a happy occasion, when many of the executives went to Wisconsin for the printing of the first issue. It was cold, but the welcome by Quad, our printer, was as warm as ever. A flag with our logo hung outside the printing plant. At a lavish dinner at his home Quad CEO Harry Quadracci toasted me but neglected to include kudos for my husband, who stormed out of the room. We had an explosive fight, but he didn't follow up on his threat to leave for the airport. (This was not a new conflict; we'd previously fought over my first draft of the publisher's letter in the first issue, in which I'd thanked my husband but not made the magazine appear our joint product. Like Chamberlain in England before me, I wrongfully thought appeasement could work, and rewrote the letter.)

The next morning was snowy. My husband and I were driving to the plant when our car was broadsided by a young man who had ignored a stop sign; I knew that no one who'd seen the previous night's tantrum would ever believe the accident wasn't my husband's fault. The car was totaled, but apart from whiplash and a bad marriage, we were fine.

Although I was unclear in 1986 about whether to stay in my marriage, I had no lack of clarity about whether my husband deserved a role in the business. The decision didn't require a choice between business and marriage, as I claimed to myself at the time. It required action on what I knew was right, and I avoided it. It could have been fatal to my partnership with Time, and to the venture. When all the facts, and your gut, lead you to a decision, you need to make it, whatever the short-term costs.

NAKED TRUTH #20

**Many business ethics decisions are in the gray area, with arguments on both sides.
In the end, you need to do what makes your gut feel good.**

Tough decisions usually have equally compelling arguments on both sides; I usually preach that close calls mean that you can't go too far wrong, except by indecision. However, close ethical calls usually have a very wrong answer. Now is the time to use every tool at your disposal—brainstorming with a friend, imagining your feelings after making each choice, making a list—to make sure you hear the message from your gut.

In 1992 I shouldn't have been distracted by the goings-on at Time Inc., as *Parenting* was part of Time Inc. Ventures (TIV), a division that ran separately from the main magazines (*People, Sports Illustrated, Fortune, Time, Money, Entertainment Weekly,* and *Life*). But the strife in New York was hard to ignore: Two of the corporation's leaders, formerly close friends, were at war. Advertising sales for the core Time Inc. properties had been centralized, and the turf battles were taking precedence over business, which was in a recession, to make it even worse. The real struggle wasn't over the approach to ad sales; it was to determine who would be the next CEO of Time Inc. Various of my New York–based friends confided their misery to me. Time Inc. was a difficult place to leave, but some of the best and brightest were preparing to do that, so disgusted were they by the internecine wars.

My then boss, Don Logan, and I had dinner in early 1992 and discussed the madness in New York. I mused aloud that maybe I should call Time Warner CEO Jerry Levin and clue him in as to the real story. A month or two went by, and one day I picked up the phone to hear Don say, without much preamble, "You remember when you were thinking about calling Jerry about what's going on in New York?" I remembered, although I had done nothing about it. "I think you should call him now." Without wasting any time wondering why Don was resurrecting my idle musings of several months back, I got on the phone.

I told Jerry that I felt very disloyal talking about Chris Meigher, because I wouldn't be a part of Time Inc. if it hadn't been for him. However, I had suffered when I reported to him, and I knew that his current direct reports (people reporting directly to him) suffered in just the same way. I told Jerry the names of several people who would tell him their experiences—if he called; they would never initiate a call to him as I was doing. If Chris became CEO, I believed politics would have a priority over results. Talent would be kept back if the person were seen as a threat. Jerry said that one of his biggest puzzlements about Chris had been the hiring of the then CEO at Sunset. I shared my perspective that it was Chris's way of keeping Don Logan from amassing any more responsibility. Jerry asked my opinion of Don, and I said he was the best boss I'd ever had, someone I had learned so much from and whom I respected totally. Jerry replied, "Yes, I think Don could run anything."

When I reported on the conversation to Don, he said— if he didn't use the word "shucks," he came close—"You don't think Jerry is thinking of me for a New York job, do you?" When he was appointed president of Time Inc. two weeks later, and Chris's departure from the company after twenty years was announced, I wondered if Don had been somewhat disingenuous with me.

What troubled me most about interfering in Time Inc. politics was being disloyal to Chris, the man who had brought me to the company. I was comforted by the knowledge that I had no personal stake in Chris's status; I no longer reported to him, so his fortunes didn't directly affect me, and it never occurred to me that my friend Don Logan would be promoted in his place. Don's advancement coincided with advancement for me, although the two were unrelated. If I could have predicted that, I probably wouldn't have made the call. I didn't think much before dialing the phone, because someone I trusted was telling me to call someone I adored. Yet if my call played a part in Don's unlikely ascension, I know now that following my gut was right, as his decade of leadership transformed Time Inc. culture and profits.

NAKED TRUTH #21

When something happens that doesn't sit well in the pit of your stomach, don't forget that feeling even if the circumstances have changed. The feeling is real; the change in circumstances may not be.

I was an established senior executive at Time, running Sunset Publishing, with my successor at *Parenting* continuing to report to me when I was dropped from the distribution list of a management meeting scheduled for a resort in the Adirondacks.

My counterparts were invited; my boss insisted it was an oversight and I shouldn't worry about it. I said it was unacceptable to me to be excluded, and needed to know promptly whether I would be invited because I needed to make childcare arrangements. My boss snapped, "So do I, Robin." I didn't respond that it is different for a nursing mother than for a man with older children and a wife who worked part-time and had live-in help. I received my invitation, and I got to spend my first Mother's Day at a corporate retreat. I thought the invitation ended my problems.

I left my seven-month-old son with his two grandmothers in my New York apartment. I went to the heliport, where Jerry Levin was picking up a number of us West Coast–based people for the trip up to the Adirondacks. I arrived early, as always, and soon Jerry's limo arrived. He chose to stay in the car until the helicopter arrived: This felt very different from his behavior a year earlier, when he'd rubbed my pregnant belly in front of a conference room of executives. Proving my Olympian powers of denial, I thought this was a reflection of changes in him, rather than in how I was regarded.

You must be wondering why you are reading advice from a woman who could miss such obvious signs. This is how I learned not to miss them.

NAKED TRUTH #22

Pay extra attention when a colleague makes an observation about your leadership or performance, especially when it is inappropriate, disturbing, or out of character.

After the meeting, I was given my fourth boss in the four years that I'd been a Time Inc. executive. Jim Nelson and I had worked as peers for years, and I respected his intelligence and drive. We were culturally far apart: He lived in Birmingham, Alabama, and after a midlife divorce had dyed his hair purplish black, gotten a bad facelift, and broken his wrist hang gliding. But I prided myself on being able to work with anyone who was smart and results-oriented, and he certainly was both.

To introduce Jim to the Sunset staff I invited him to sit in on an employee task force that had been formed to address the subject of book/magazine cooperation; his company, Southern Progress, had done wonders in this area. He hadn't yet met the senior Sunset editors—that meeting was scheduled for later in the day—but I don't follow a lot of formalities, and Jim had been around Sunset many times before getting responsibility for the division. The task force happened to be all female, ranging from middle-management to junior.

It hadn't occurred to me that a senior executive would first voice his complaints to such an audience, but Jim did not have a positive word to say about Sunset, and was vocal in his criticism of Sunset's food coverage. He kept repeating, wagging his stubby finger, "What women want is recipes." It was his first appearance with Sunset employees and seemed designed to exacerbate their fears that he would try to make *Sunset* into *Southern Living*, the magazine he'd run before being promoted to his new corporate position. I was struck by the fact that a man in 1994 didn't know that he couldn't tell a group of women what women want. Within fifteen minutes of the end of this meeting, Sunset's executive editor told me she feared for my future.

For this editor to have voiced an opinion about her boss's boss's future was a very strong statement. I didn't miss it. This time, I listened to my gut.

I flew to New York to have dinner with Don Logan, Time Inc. CEO. I was now several layers removed from Don, but we were still close. He told me we could keep the dinner secret, but I followed my nature, which is not secretive. On

Don's recommendation, I told Jim Nelson's boss that the only way I would try to work for Jim would be if I had an employment contract. This was contrary to Time Inc. policy at the time; Don was trying to do away with contracts, as he (rightly) saw them as the floor to any future negotiation. But I was given a contract that would last for twelve months: If during that period Jim fired me or I wanted to resign for good reasons, I would get two years' severance. After the term of the contract, my status would revert to regular employment. With the tacit acknowledgment that Time Inc. management understood the difficult situation in which I'd been placed, I moved forward, having read the clues and protected myself.

NAKED TRUTH #23

When something is written in black and white, or even in an email, it should be harder to ignore.

I told myself the rational reasons why I could work for Jim. I only wanted to stay with Sunset another year or two, as the company's return to profitability would then be in full gear and I could consider it an unpleasant success; clearly the company valued me, or they wouldn't have given me an expensive employment guarantee; if Jim were truly gunning for me, he could have resisted my contract. Rationally, I could convince myself that everything was going to work out. One piece of paper, however, ended my rationalizations.

Jim presented me with his handwritten list of things to change about Sunset. It included precise dates for such changes as an increase in type size, binding (from glue to sta-ple), number of recipes per issue, and number of columns per page. None of the ideas was particularly disagreeable—in fact, I agreed with (and was already implementing) most of them. But after years of running a successful company I was dispirited and depressed to have a boss who would think I needed this kind of guidance and micromanagement. The handwriting wasn't just on Jim's list; it was on the wall.

So if you have managed to ignore your queasy stomach, failed to pay attention to warnings from your colleagues, and lulled yourself with a list of rational reasons why bad things are not going to happen, a written message can still stand out. Don't file it, don't put it into the garbage or into a folder on your desktop. Keep it in front of your face until you have dealt with the problem.

NAKED TRUTH #24

"Strategy" is an off-putting word that can muffle messages from your gut.

Your gut is valuable not just in guiding your career, but in making the most strategic decisions. The biggest strategic blunders are made when leaders don't do a gut check: *Will it work?*

I'm not sure I know the difference between a strategy and a tactic, except that in some business circles the way to dash a plan is to claim it's tactical instead of strategic. And I am sure that strategy without tactics is doomed, but not vice versa. Whether strategic or tactical, though, your gut is invaluable.

I had joined CNET, one of the first Internet companies to go public, in 1997. At an Internet company during those giddy years the most important strategic decision was how to use your soaring stock to acquire companies to accelerate your growth. There were so many deals to do: The challenge was to decide which ones. As a newcomer to CNET's executive team, I was playing catch-up and had almost nothing except my gut for guidance. One of the inexperienced but Internet-savvy managers exploded in frustration to me about his inability to convince the founders to make a particular acquisition. I'd seen enough of this twenty-eight-year-old to believe that he knew the business, if not how to express himself, so I convinced the founders to revisit the idea. We made the most important acquisition in our company's short life, and to this day I could barely describe to you what software it involved.

There are likely to be areas of your company that remain foreign to you. Yet they can be of key strategic importance, and rather than be intimidated by your lack of technical knowledge, you should feel freed to follow your instincts about people.

FOUR

Mentors and AntImentors

T HE M WORD THAT DIVIDES WOMEN EXECUTIVES IS NOT Motherhood, it's Mentor. Some of us believe fervently in the mentors we've had, and some believe equally fervently that the search for mentors is a giant waste of energy. The only consensus is that formal mentoring programs are a joke.

To me, the search for a mentor is like the search for a perfect mate. If you are looking for someone with whom you have eternal chemistry, share all important values, and whose personal habits will remain endearing through the decades, you may be searching a long time and missing out on some great partners along the way. The two men who came closest to being my mentor turned out to fail in the arena most important to me—ethics—yet I still learned a tremendous amount from each of them.

Early in my career, before I'd heard the M word, I picked up valuable lessons from men and women with whom I couldn't identify at all. Yet there was learning to be had:

- Kathy Keeton, the former "dancer" (probably stripper) who lived with *Penthouse* founder Bob Guccione, overcame almost pathological shyness to run advertising sales for the magazine. This probably was similar to stripping for a shy person, but showed that you can succeed despite any personality trait. For me, I have trouble with confrontation with my loved ones, but no one has accused me of that trait in the workplace.
- *Penthouse*'s CFO protected every dollar of the company's money as if it were his own. I learned from him, and expect the same values from employees.
- The *Penthouse* circulation director demonstrated that it can be more effective to disarm people with easygoing charm than to hit them over the heads with your brains and dedication. I'm not particularly charming, but I try not to be heavy-handed.
- *Penthouse*'s head of public relations had exquisite personal taste and finely tuned ethics. Impeccable in Sonia Rykiel, she devotedly represented a tasteless magazine. I learned I could be dedicated to a product that didn't appeal to me personally.

I could no more wear Sonia Rykiel than I could take my clothes off in public, but my on-the-job training had begun, as I picked and chose what to learn from these somewhat unlikely (and unaware) mentors. After three decades of that training I am convinced that "the mentor" is a very rare animal, but if you are curious about how people succeed in business and pay attention, your job performance will be improved.

Once a mentor, not always a mentor.

Sometimes the people who teach you the most can prove terrible role models as time goes on. When I became general manager of *Mother Jones* I was woefully unprepared for the sophisticated circulation techniques on which the magazine depended. I was fortunate that the longtime circulation consultant, John Klingel, was an excellent teacher; I soon joined the ranks of Klingel Klones, as we called ourselves—circulation directors at a variety of his client publishers who followed his methodologies religiously.

Because John had worked at Time Inc. he would have been a natural guide as I entered that world, but a rift quickly developed between us. John was also a consultant to *Hippocrates,* another magazine launched in 1986. The rift began in 1988, when I received a call from a venture capitalist asking my opinion of *Hippocrates* as an investment; he said that John had given me as a reference. Because of my partnership with Time Inc. and heavy media exposure, my opinion mattered in the venture capital world. I tried to be as positive as I honestly could be—*Hippocrates'*s launch had been abysmal on the advertising front, and I had been unimpressed with the magazine despite the editorial accolades it had received. I then called John and gently chided him for not having given me advance notice that he wanted me as a reference, I could have done a better job with preparation. Another venture capitalist called, but this time I was ready and was a stronger ally. Then, to my astonishment, my boss at Time told me he was considering an investment in *Hippocrates.* I was furious and went to dinner with John to tell him what a breach of ethics I considered this: By getting me to hype the investment to venture capitalists, in theory he was increasing the price Time would have to pay for its investment. (In reality this didn't occur, as the venture capitalists were uninterested.) I felt he had put me—without my knowledge—into a compromised position. But it was as if we were speaking different languages. John thought my concern was ridiculous. It was not the last time we would clash over ethics, but it was the last time I looked to him as more than a technical expert. Luckily for me, before my disillusionment I had been trained in circulation by one of the best in the business.

It will doubtless be painful when you realize that your erstwhile mentor has nothing more to teach you. But it's worse than painful if you don't cut your losses. No one's perfect, so no one can be your mentor in every area of business. Emulate the good stuff and determine to be different from the bad.

NAKED TRUTH #26

Choose your teachers based on talent and personal connection, not upon hierarchy or shared gender.

A logical place to look for mentors would have been among senior women of Time Inc., but most of them were my peers, or junior to me. Although I was Time Inc.'s first female publisher, I didn't really count, as *Parenting* was a joint venture. I was quickly joined by Lisa Valk, publisher of *Life*, and Ann Moore, founding publisher of *SI for Kids*. The three of us shared a wonderful lunch at the Rainbow Room, where I suggested we form the Girl Publishers Union. Although I learned from both of them, they were oil and water: Both Harvard Business School grads, Lisa was all Southern gentility and manners; Ann spoke her mind and had a reputation as "too individualistic." Lisa was all about style and process; Ann was about results. Ann was incredibly creative, sensible, and funny; the company had done handstands to deny her the job she should have been given, as publisher of *Sports Illustrated*, and made her founding publisher of *SI for Kids* instead. Today she is CEO of Time Inc., and got that job position because her results were so good that she couldn't be denied any longer. I identified with her much more than Lisa, but while it's possible to get support (and great gossip) from peers, advice is trickier.

I found people to learn from in unlikely places. Just after *Parenting*'s launch, at an American Booksellers convention in May 1987, I introduced myself to Don Logan, then the CEO of Southern Progress, a Birmingham-based company Time had acquired several years earlier. I was curious about the leader of a company that was entrepreneurial, culturally unique within Time Inc., and highly profitable. *Parenting* had the first two characteristics, and as it grew I wanted to be sure it had the third. My first impression of Don reveals my innate prejudice against Southerners, because I thought he was a good old boy around whom I could dance circles. It took about ten minutes before I realized that this was one of the smartest people I'd ever met. He might have been twice my size and from a different planet culturally, but I recognized true business greatness long before Time Inc. did. While I quickly bonded with my female peers, often in a corporation the people at your level can't or won't offer assistance. You may have little to learn from them. When you find someone who is more experienced and accomplished, as Don was in comparison to me, and willing to spend time with you—grab the opportunity.

On the surface, I was more comfortable with Lisa and Ann, my female peers. But Don's results made me look past his facade and listen past his drawl. If someone in your organization has created a division, or a project, or a departmental culture that you admire, look to the results, not the style.

NAKED TRUTH #27

Temporarily out-of-favor and very senior people may have more time for you. Since you are looking for learning, not self-promotion, don't stand on ceremony.

Jerry Levin eventually became CEO of Time Warner, but in the mid-eighties I don't think he had any direct reports. He'd given up running HBO, but he was still a top executive, and called Time Inc.'s "resident genius." I was immediately drawn to this brilliant, self-deprecating man, and the friendship was sealed when we realized we shared May 6 as a birthday—along with a fascination with others born that day (Willie Mays and Sigmund Freud, most famously, and Jerry's son and Carol Smith, most emotionally). Soon he would be a regular lunch date on my New York trips, and someone who made me feel comfortable calling him to weigh in, say, on the choice of CFO. He would give me advice on how to handle my boss, and my boss's boss.

Because of my friendship with Jerry, in 1990 I was asked to look into the feasibility of a magazine idea Quincy Jones had. I was partnered with Gil Rogin, the former editor of *Sports Illustrated* and now a legend, but biding the last days of his career in a meaningless corporate editor job on the 34th floor.

When I met Gil in his office I was struck by the photo of him, notebook in hand, interviewing Muhammed Ali, along with the drying Speedos draped across a trophy. His assistant proved the rule I'd learned early: You can learn much about an executive by his/her assistant; she was attractive, unfailingly gracious, competent, and irreverent; when Gil was acting like a lunatic, she let him know (privately, usually), but she defended him loyally.

Gil's years at Time Inc. had made him a wealthy although never satisfied man. He was a great example to me: Passion and personal idiosyncrasy could live for decades, even in an arid political environment. And most significantly, his corporate exile gave him the time as well as the emotional need to be a mentor to me.

I remain proud of the speech I gave celebrating Gil at his black-tie retirement dinner, and the opener became rather talked about: "I am really honored to be the only woman speaking at this event, and to tell you something about Gil you probably don't know. Human Resources surveyed the women of Time Inc. and asked whom they rated highest as a mentor, and Gil was at the top of the list. So because of that I want to tell you about Gil's record as a feminist. (*Pause while I look at their bored expressions.*) Then I realized, wait, am I really going to get up in front of two hundred people who *know* him and call Gil a feminist? After all, this is the man who, when I said I was nervous about tonight's speech, said, 'Don't worry, Robin, just show them your tits.' (*Stunned silence, then roar of laughter.*) On our first business lunch, Gil kissed me good-bye on the lips. And he's been that kind of a mentor ever since." Because I had learned from Gil about being true to myself I could refer to my tits in front of two hundred people, and treasure the memory.

When women ask me to mentor them I have to say I find it a false process when done deliberately. The most valuable lessons I have learned came from observing behavior in the office—and vowing to do things differently when I got a chance.

My best mentors have been antimentors, the men whose behavior taught me what not to do. They may be antimentors, but I am not antimen. Some of my best friends, and everyone I have ever slept with, are men. I'm sure it's coincidental that the worst people I've experienced in business are men too.

Here are two of the bad boys who taught me so much.

Chris Meigher had been the executive at Time Inc. whose cool, smart questions convinced me in our first meeting that this publishing company was the right partner for the launch of *Parenting*. He was my partner in the joint venture, and became my boss upon the sale. The years of partnership forced me to be more independent than would have been my nature, as Chris quickly made it clear that he didn't want to hear any bad news—I was on my own to figure it out. As a boss, he showed traits that I became resolved to never emulate:

- **Lack of direct feedback.** When I became an "official Time Incer" after the sale I joined the company's Annual Incentive Plan—a bonus that, depending on performance, was initially set at a target of 50 percent of my base salary. In February 2001, when the bonuses were awarded, Chris met with me to review my performance (against goals I was then hearing for the first time); he went through the grading system, and after a half hour I was left with no idea whether or not he was pleased with my performance. I mentioned this to Lisa Valk, and she said, "You got a 132, right?" I didn't know how she knew this confidential data point. "He gives everyone 132."

  I resolved to spend the time giving my team candid and thorough feedback, and not to wait for the annual review.

- **Form over function.** No matter the size or complexity or needs of the business, Chris structured our reports to him exactly the same way. We would have group meetings, and the same amount of time would be allocated to the head of a small, money-losing start-up as to the head of the group that produced *all* the profits for Chris's division. The message was clear: Your importance was measured by less objective factors. It kept everyone in our places.

  I resolved to manage from the bottom up, responding to the needs of the business (or department, or direct report).

- **Politics over performance.** His rules of appropriate corporate behavior were hinted at, but not said directly. They were not a helpful or even other-directed set of instructions, which might have introduced me to the mysterious protocols of Time Inc. His motivation was all about his own standing: If a rival's magazine was quoted in the *New York Times,* he would querulously ask why *Parenting*'s profile wasn't higher; if I chatted too openly with another executive, his forbidding secretary would instantly and wordlessly convey my trespass even while Chris's set expression didn't waver.

I became careful to separate my desire for a problem-free execution of our plan from the needs of the business—which always has problems. My team had to be able to tell me without fear.

Although much of this book reflects my belief that bringing your personal self into the business arena is the best, most effective way to lead, if you are an egomaniac it's probably best to park that persona at the office door. The last bad boy in my Time Warner career taught me:

- **Ego-driven decisions are the wrong ones.** Jim Nelson is brilliant. But he is so impressed with that fact that he can't make room for other people's ideas. When my successor at *Parenting,* Carol Smith, resigned in the middle of the magazine's most profitable year, her second-in-command, Anne Welch, was the logical choice to take her place. But when Carol gave notice, Jim began to act like a petulant teenager whose girlfriend had decided to go to the prom with someone else. I sent a note (two years after I'd left the company) to Jim's boss, Don Logan, saying, "I am not sure if the founder's thoughts on succession are relevant, but would be happy to share them if you are interested." Don called, and we had a long conversation. At the end, he said, "I know Jim would do just the opposite if he knew the advice were coming from you." I wished Don well. It didn't take long for me to hear the result of my call. The next day, Jim sputtered with rage, "Don Logan isn't going to tell me who is going to be president of *Parenting*." The man Jim chose was the head of newsstand sales at *People*. He and Anne had begun their Time Inc. careers at the same time, in the same precise position; over the decade-plus since then, she repeatedly had been promoted to higher positions than he had. Don chose not to prevent a moral wrong from being committed in the name of giving autonomy to one of his people. The man chosen to lead *Parenting* lasted fewer than two years. I had stopped reading the magazine I had given birth to a decade earlier. I have never looked at another copy.

FIVE

Doing the Right Thing

BUSINESS HEROICS ARE MUCH MORE INTERESTING THAN everyday rescues from fires, drowning, car wrecks. Because you can usually get away without doing the right thing. No one will notice. So it demands a moral compass that jumping into the river after a drowning child doesn't.

My guess is that the businesspeople accused of white-collar crimes—from Enron's Andrew Fastow to Worldcom's Scott Sullivan—had, at many earlier times in their careers where they had moral choices to make, made the easy and wrong one, were not detected, and went on to bigger crimes. Whether you agreed with the government's decision to prosecute Martha Stewart, or the outcome, I find it striking that everyone I spoke with who had worked with her had no doubt that she would lie and think herself above the law. I would hope and expect that if I were in her position my colleagues would give me the benefit of the doubt.

While it's probably good news that business ethics are

now taught in school, that is a tad late. Did your parents teach you not to lie? Did they teach you moral priorities, that someone's sick child is more important than their report deadline? Did you learn early from your siblings not to unfairly enrich yourself at others' expense? Sometimes it's subtle—how you learned that playing fair means sometimes not playing by the rules. If you had a childhood full of these types of lessons, you will have a moral compass in business as long as you remember that there is no dividing line between business and personal morality. If you lacked these lessons from your parents, play catch-up now.

NAKED TRUTH #29

Wood-paneled, book-lined law offices can make the words spoken there seem thoughtful and authoritative— that's the point of the decor.

Forget your surroundings. I have been amazed at some of the low-life behavior I have witnessed in fancy offices. When I was starting *Parenting* one of my seed investors was the venture partnership of an august law firm. Time often used that law firm for legal matters in San Francisco, but because of the conflict of interest they used another firm on my deal. When Time stipulated that they would not invest in *Parenting* unless the seed investors accepted a three-times-their-investment buyout, the law firm's venture-partners asked to see me with the magazine's general counsel, Themis Michos, another seed investor.

The venture-partners had figured out a very complex

structure that would enable them to sell their partnership interests to Time but then carry some sort of phantom equity in the company. They assured me this would meet Time's concerns. The legal intricacies were over my head and I didn't try to understand them. (You usually don't need to understand the technical stuff.) I agreed that I would take the proposal to Time. Oh no, they said quickly, you wouldn't need to disclose this arrangement to Time; it would just be between us. Now I didn't need to think about legal intricacies. I didn't even look at Themis. "I am sure that if you are proposing this," I said, "it's technically legal, but there is no way I am going to start my partnership with Time keeping this kind of thing secret."

My heart was pounding, and I was so stunned that I can't even remember their response, but Themis and I left quickly. I waited until after the deal with Time was signed, then called Time's general counsel to let him know what his law firm's venture-partners had proposed. I hope and believe that they never worked for Time again.

I am not recommending that you act as I do, choosing to get involved because I didn't want to see this law firm continue to benefit from the company some of their partners had wanted to mislead. That was my sense of morality (and possibly vengeance). But I am recommending that you follow your moral compass. You can't participate in something you know to be wrong; you then need to choose whether to be a silent nonparticipant or to make noise, whichever feels true to you.

NAKED TRUTH #30

You can learn, and benefit, from others' ethical lapses.

An episode from *Parenting*'s early days remains as clear to me as this morning's breakfast. And the taste is as bitter as the coffee dregs in my sink. Our San Francisco offices were being built. Suddenly we needed to hire an editorial staff, but we had no place to put them. Thirteen people filled every crevice of our Buena Vista Park Victorian. Pac Bell couldn't fit in enough phone lines; the technician fell through the ceiling in the attempt, leaving a gaping hole. (He was unhurt.) On the wall beneath the gaping hole was a huge brown splash painting created by Eileen Rivkin, our ad salesperson, sliding down the flight of stairs holding her coffee cup. Aristotle, our German short-haired pointer, chased his tail.

Everyone needed me—to make a sales call, a speech, go to a Time Inc. meeting, have lunch, dinner, a cup of coffee, go to Chicago, to Vermont. The receptionist gave me stacks of message slips with calls to return. Somehow I found time to buy a new car; Eileen had convinced me that my nine-year-old Toyota Corolla was unsuitable for my new station in life. "You can't pick up Time Inc. executives at the airport in that. First of all, you can't be dealing with a stick shift. And the bumper sticker has got to go." She approved the choice of a Toyota Cressida, as the company was on her target list of accounts; "The Moral Majority is Neither" bumper sticker was lost in the transition.

My husband kept a list in his Day-Timer, which he always had with him, even in his robe. I asked employees not to arrive before 7:30 so I could be sure I'd have time to get off the phone with *Parenting*'s New York–based publisher Carol Smith, shower, and dress first.

To top it off, I had recently received a letter from Gruner & Jahr, publishers of *Parents*, informing me that they intended to sue us for trademark infringement.

That was not the surprising news. I had consulted with a trademark expert who'd assured me that *Parents* was not a defensible mark, and that Gruner & Jahr had not protected it in the past enough to help their cause. Time Inc.'s view had been the same. However, what our expert neglected to mention was that Gruner & Jahr could attempt to obtain a temporary restraining order, which could delay our publication date and probably put us out of business.

My father called from New York in the middle of the day. He'd never done that before. I took the call in the dining room, where four people were working at the table. "It's probably nothing, doll, but there's this very little—as small as you can see on an X-ray—spot on my lung. It has to come out, but the doctor doesn't think there is anything to worry about because I haven't smoked in so many years. The surgery is next week."

Had the room gone silent or did the buzzing in my ears drown everyone out? I cannot do this, I cannot be three thousand miles from my family. I cannot be the leader who's strong, cannot be optimistic. I start to hear sounds again, my husband is asking me, What happened? What did he say? Don't touch me, don't hug me, don't try to comfort me.

I walked to the back of the house, sitting on the wooden steps so I could be alone and look east over the city, toward New York.

I called the president of Gruner & Jahr, John Beni, to ask to move the date of our meeting in New York to discuss the impending suit by one day, as my father's surgery was scheduled for that precise time. He refused, earning his permanent place in my Hall of Shame.

The meeting was a complete waste of time, as Beni was unprepared to move from his position that we could not use the name *Parenting* unless it was preceded by a modifier (*American Parenting, Modern Parenting,* etc.). His secretary interrupted once with a note saying that my father had come through the surgery. Meanwhile, a pleasant summer day had turned to rain. Beni paraded me through the *Parents* offices like a prisoner of war, asking people if they had an umbrella to give "this young lady." I could barely be civil as I raced out of the offices to Penn Station. Of course there were no cell phones in 1986, so it was not until I arrived at the hospital and saw my ashen sister waiting for me in the lobby that I learned it was cancer.

The doctors let me see my father in the recovery room, and he awoke long enough to ask me, "Do we get to keep the name?" I said something more positive than I felt (the first cancer lie).

The trademark issue was the first big problem my new partners and I faced. Tension mounted: Don Spurdle of Time and I thought that adding a modifier (*American Parenting, Modern Parenting,* etc.) would be acceptable, although not optimal, so *Parenting*'s top executives tried to come up with a long list of possible names; the Time executives farther away from the issue flatly insisted that *Parenting* was the name we would use and I should be able to figure out a solution to this problem. I ran into Time Inc.'s editor-in-chief, Henry Grunwald, in an elevator, and when he asked for an update on the name thing, gave him my view that a modifier wouldn't be that bad; he responded, "I like simple magazine names. *Time. Life. People.*" The doors closed behind him, and I was frantic.

With decades of hindsight, I realize that John Beni's response to my request for a twenty-four-hour delay was not just an ethical lapse for him, but a business misstep. He fueled my determination to crush his magazine (today *Parenting* is larger than *Parents,* which had a seventy-five-year head start). At a time when my energy might have sagged because of my personal crisis, I was motivated anew. When you witness terrible behavior by a competitor, even if it is a momentary setback for you, you can turn it into an advantage. If they are doing this to you, imagine what they do to their own people. They are unwittingly providing a window into their leadership problems; use the opportunity.

NAKED TRUTH #31

Inept cheating makes matters worse. So even if your moral code permits cheating, refrain on practical grounds.

We got a lucky break. In the middle of our legal strategizing my trademark lawyer called, breathless. *Parents* had taken a booklet called *"Parents'* Problem Solver," slapped a new cover on it, called it "Parenting: The Problem Solver," used our logo design, and attempted to register the trademark. They hadn't even bothered to change the inner sixty-four pages, which were already printed. My lawyer was both shocked and gleeful. She had never seen something this blatant, and was confident it would enrage the judge assigned to our case. She was confident that Gruner & Jahr's clumsy attempt would eliminate any chance we'd had of losing the suit.

In the end, none of the legal maneuvering solved the problem. Chris Meigher (who'd green-lighted *Parenting* for Time) also had responsibility for *Fortune,* which had a $20 million–plus printing contract with Brown Printing, which was owned by another division of Gruner & Jahr. It required Chris's diplomatic skills and communication back to headquarters (in the Black Forest of Germany), but we reached a settlement that involved no money, granted our right to use the name (as long as the design didn't resemble *Parents*) forever, and did not tie *Fortune's* continued printing to the case's resolution. Soon after, John Beni left Gruner & Jahr.

I had learned a few lessons. John Beni, of course, was right to oppose our use of the name. I also learned that when a lawyer is saying what you want to hear (that you would win a lawsuit), you also need to ask about its possible path (timing and expense). And, finally, capitulation for the sake of expeditiousness is not the right path; *Parenting* was a much better name than any alternative we had.

Most importantly, I realized that doing the right thing is justified not just on moral grounds, but practical ones. Gruner & Jahr did the wrong thing, and got caught. Long before Rosie O'Donnell sued them (and vice versa), they demonstrated a corporate culture of a willingness to cheat. Most people don't cheat well. So do the right thing, whether for the right or the expeditious reason.

NAKED TRUTH #32

When the stakes are enormous and the pressure is intense, even a normally ethical person can make a mistake.

When you are under extra pressure and need to make an important decision, try to take a deep breath and think twice, or three times. It's easy to slip.

I myself came close to doing something shameful. I tell you about it, despite my embarrassment, to demonstrate how easy it is to slip. A clause in my partnership with Time established benchmarks for the magazine's performance within its first six months of publication. Failure to meet the circulation benchmark would lead to draconian consequences, including Time taking majority ownership of the magazine for almost no money and being enabled to replace me. The results of the first direct-mail campaign suggested we would miss the subscription-order benchmark. I dutifully told this to Don Spurdle, who said (perhaps without the meaning I ascribed to his words): "It would be ridiculous to invoke the benchmark penalties if you just miss a little; don't let that happen." So my husband and I had an elaborate plan to defraud the system by holding onto packages returned by the post office as undeliverable, which we would then mail in as fake orders, complete with money orders. These would count as paid subscriptions.

I wish I could say that my moral compass stopped me before committing this fraud, but the only reason we didn't go through with it was that it became clear that it wouldn't be a near miss: The shortfall was going to be significant. If I had done the wrong thing, not only would it have been futile (we would have missed the benchmarks anyway), but the most deeply satisfying adventure of my career would be tainted. And, of course, if we'd been caught, my career would likely have been over.

Don't overlook a potential corporate hero just because he wears a suit.

Corporate heroes are often unlikely—they don't look like firefighters. Almost every woman I interviewed had a story about a colleague coming to her rescue. When *Parenting* was first staffing up in 1986, I needed to find a health plan for our about to be hired twenty-seven employees. Since we couldn't afford the Time Inc. benefits plan, I shopped for coverage. The complicating factor was our executive editor's son, who had been born with a hole in his heart. Lucien had already had several major surgeries and would need more. I couldn't find a health plan willing to underwrite our small group without excluding pre-existing conditions. That would have meant that we couldn't hire David Markus as our founding executive editor.

I went to Ken Saum, the head of benefits for Time Inc. I remember him as the kind of methodical and dry man you would expect in that position. He agreed to convince (or coerce) one of Time's insurance suppliers to put us on a plan that wouldn't exclude pre-existing conditions. The catch was that it had a $1 million cap on coverage, but Ken assured me that in Time's twenty-thousand–employee history, no one had come close to using a million dollars in benefits. Really sick people just don't live that long, and chronic illnesses don't have heavy hospitalizations.

Several years later David and his wife, Daphne Larkin, told me that Lucien's medical bills had approached $885,000.

They were doing what they could to cut back on nursing costs, but were frightened that the cap was in sight.

I went to New York to see Ken Saum for the first time in years, and told him that the magazine was approaching breakeven and I would like to improve the employees' benefits. He agreed and started talking about all the things we didn't have that employees would welcome: dental coverage, disability, employer contributions to their 401(k). I told him, "Actually, Ken, I think removing the $1 million cap on our health coverage would be the best employee benefit change." Ken immediately nodded and said he could see that that would be in the best interest of our employees. I still get a tear in my eye thinking of the compassion of this seemingly dry bureaucrat, but that was the kind of company Time was.

I tell the story about Ken Saum to show an unlikely hero, and to urge you to look for other corporate heroes—people really can rise to the occasion, and successful leaders all tell similar stories, which only happen when you ask for help.

There is another, more complex story here about ethics in decision making. By choosing to put our company resources into a health plan that would just help one employee's family, I probably did a disservice to the other employees, who still lacked some basic benefits. Being a CEO means making lonely decisions: I took money out of employees' pockets to protect one employee from sure catastrophe. I wouldn't ask the employees for their vote on the matter, but judging from their turnout at Lucien's funeral several years later, I know they would have made the same choice.

Your decisions about mundane policies that affect employees daily—from expense accounts to office/cubicle design—will affect your success more than your five-year strategic plan.

A leader establishes the moral climate of her sphere of influence—from a group to a department to a company—in many small steps. Just because they are small, though, doesn't mean they should get less of your attention.

Little decisions ended up establishing the culture at *Parenting* long before I was aware that "culture" was something a company has. For example, I believe in as many private offices as the budget can afford; people like them. Windows on the interior walls of those offices let light into the center of the offices, and even the most spacious private offices only had room for a three- or four-person meeting. Most important to me, my office was in the middle of the action, not in a corner. We all flew coach. (On a rare flight to our San Francisco office, Don Spurdle insisted on flying "in the back of the bus" with me, so I couldn't "do that self-righteous entrepreneur thing" and make fun of Time Inc.'s ostentatious expense accounts. He got his revenge by smoking many cigarettes, which were still allowed on planes in those days.) We encouraged people to add a Saturday night to their business trips, picking up their hotel and meal expenses if they did so, if that worked out to be cheaper than the higher airfare of a Friday return. Of course, we flew on weekends whenever we could, so as not to lose a precious workday.

When I declined the superior executive benefits package that Time Warner offered, because I believe that CEOs should have the same benefits as their employees—in particular, not be given a lower deductible on health coverage for their families—I assumed I was just making a personal choice for myself. (In retrospect, I should have lobbied, as I had the top executives' ears, to change the policy.) However, there are few secrets at a company, and even a private decision like this has a way of filtering out to some employees and contributing to the tone of the company. Doesn't everyone sort of know which executives pad their expense accounts? And whether the company has uniform standards for how employees are treated, or different ones for favored people? Employees take their clues from lots of places, and repay the company for its ethics or lack of them.

NAKED TRUTH #35

If you make a costly gesture in order to earn others' gratitude, you've wasted your money: Most will feel entitled to, or forget, the generosity. But if you do it because it's the right thing, you will always be rewarded.

Doing the right thing is easier if you are not driven by financial gain. I was put to the test in 1989 when, after three years of publication, the magazine was getting close to breakeven—in fact, we could have broken even that year if we'd wished. Every dollar Time invested came directly out of my pocket. However, for the magazine to reach its full potential it needed continued investment, which would have a great return for the business if not for me personally. At each of these crossroads—whenever an investment decision needed to be made—I chose the path that benefited the business.

Soon after my divorce was final I made an ethical decision that cost me in the short term but paid off later. I granted gifts to about a dozen *Parenting* managers who had worked for the magazine since its founding yet had had no promise of a share in the proceeds, so that upon the sale of my interest, they would receive a piece of the purchase price. I had fought with my ex-husband before our split to be able to reward a wider circle of people who had contributed to the success of the venture; once I was unencumbered by his resistance I did the right thing. Most businesspeople would have agreed with my ex-husband: The management team had not been promised anything, and had been paid competitive salaries. Granting them ownership interests might not have made financial sense, because at that point it only gave me about eighteen months of their theoretically raised commitment, and the highest-risk portion of the launch had already passed. Yet I couldn't have enjoyed my prospective riches without sharing them with those responsible. Being "unselfish" was actually in my self-interest.

You will have choices to make in business—perhaps not as expensive as this example, but choices nonetheless. If you approach the decision only from the short-term perspective, you can miss out on long-term rewards. *Parenting* is a bigger, more successful magazine today because I made the long-term investments in the early days; perhaps I wouldn't have been able to publish this book without that success. Several of the original managers from *Parenting*'s launch collaborate with me today; perhaps without sharing the magazine's success I wouldn't have their loyalty and support.

It may be a tenuous and easily overlooked connection, but some business decisions have life-and-death impact. Think about the ultimate consequence of your actions.

I am as militantly anticigarettes as anyone. Long before my father's diagnosis of lung cancer (twenty-seven years after he'd quit smoking) I had been uncomfortable with this mainstay of magazines' economics. On the one hand, as long as they are legal, I believe a manufacturer has a right to advertise its product. On the other, I don't see much difference in social benefit between cigarettes and heroin. I had been accustomed to the importance of cigarette advertising in the magazine world; since it was banned on television, manufacturers fattened publishers' wallets for many years. One of my early jobs in the advertising department, at *Penthouse,* was to log insertion orders (contracts for the appearances of ads in the magazine); the cigarette ads specified the number of pages of separation mandated between the ad and any mention of cancer or death. Kathy Keeton kept every brand of cigarette in a case in her office, carefully selecting the appropriate one to smoke when on a sales call to its manufacturer or advertising agency.

Fortunately, until late in my career I had never had to make a tough decision. I wasn't in charge of advertising at *Runner's World,* where it was a moot point anyway. *Mother Jones,* before I arrived, had wrestled with it; they accepted tobacco ads (its only significant advertising revenue, then or ever), and promptly published a cover story entitled "Tobacco: The Truth No One Else Will Print" to prove its ideological independence. Needless to say, the ads disappeared. It was an easy call to be principled at *Parenting*, as the tobacco companies wouldn't risk public wrath by targeting pregnant women—nor would that be an effective use of their advertising dollars.

When push came to shove, I didn't stand on my principles. As Time's head of magazine development in 1992 I oversaw the test of *Vibe* with founders Quincy Jones and Russell Simmons. They both thought it important that the magazine accept tobacco advertising. I was pretty sure that we would attract a large teenage audience, so the decision was especially tricky. On the one hand, revenue from those ads might make the difference as to whether the magazine could launch—and launching was a definite social good. On the other, advertising tobacco to teens is a sin. I allowed the wrong decision to be made, and I still regret it.

I should have known better, because I'd worked for a CEO who was a hero. Mel Ziegler was the founding CEO of Banana Republic and remained so after he and his wife Patricia sold the company to the Gap. It was an uneasy corporate relationship, but Banana Republic was earning so much money that the Gap gave Mel and Patricia a lot of latitude. However, Mel pushed the envelope of autonomy too far in 1988 when he learned that the building on Bluxome Street that housed Banana's headquarters was, despite the landlord's representations, not earthquake retrofit. The company had just spent over $2 million on interior improvements to the space, and in considering more structural improvements, an engineer advised Mel that it would not withstand a 5.5 quake—which are relatively common in the Bay Area. Mel issued the order: We move, and now. Because of the short timeframe—completed in two weeks—this meant moving the staff into several separate office spaces around town, and that, combined with the ensuing lawsuit from the landlord over the broken lease, infuriated the Gap, which fired Mel and Patricia soon thereafter.

The Bluxome building collapsed months later in the Loma Prieta quake, killing six people. The landlord was prosecuted criminally. The Gap never paid public tribute to Mel for saving its employees' lives.

Business heroism and cowardice usually are not mentioned. Although few people would blame me, my cowardice on cigarette advertising may have led to more deaths than Mel's bravery averted. I hope you never have as dramatic a decision as we faced, but if you do, be like Mel. Learn from my regret.

NAKED TRUTH #37

When one of your core values is challenged, you need to speak out. Loudly. Save polite demeanor for less important issues.

Vibe challenged me on many levels. Jerry Levin asked me to recommend whether to test Quincy Jones's idea for a magazine about rap music. I hadn't even heard rap at that point, but I was partnered with the legendary editor Gil Rogin, and he was a music nut. Gil and I recommended a newsstand test. It would require hiring an editor and one or two other editorial hands, but freelancers and *Parenting* staffers would do most of the work.

Time would be putting up the money and supplying the magazine expertise; Quincy would be providing oversight to be sure we were executing his vision. Tensions emerged quickly.

The first task was to find an editor. Best known as a writer, Jonathan van Meter loved the music and the culture. Gil was impressed by his editorial standards, and I adored him instantly. Quincy and Russell approved the hire, as Jonathan impressed them with his knowledge and passion.

Despite that approval, Quincy and Russell immediately began to second-guess Jonathan. Although one of their core views had been that the magazine needed to be upscale and aspirational, they found Jonathan's taste too "fancy." Soon the code word was dropped and Russell's discomfort with a gay editor's vision became open and explicit.

After one particularly difficult meeting I called Gil, and we did not have to exchange many words. "I think we have to go tell Quincy that we can't work with Russell." "I'll meet you in L.A." "If he doesn't agree, we tell Jerry we've got to pull the plug."

Quincy was almost silent while Gil and I talked. Whatever terms he reached with Russell we didn't know, but we never worked with him again. It was a tremendous relief, as I had become very involved in the concept and really wanted the test to go forward.

Around the time of the showdown with Quincy, I got a call from one of Time Inc.'s top employment lawyers. He said, "Robin, I want to talk about the issues with Jonathan van Meter; I understand there are some concerns about having a gay editor." I started ranting immediately: "I am not going to have this conversation. I don't know if being gay is a protected class, but it should be, and we shouldn't be discussing anyone's sexuality as part of their job. It's outrageous and . . ." He interrupted me as I paused for breath. "Robin, I guess you didn't know I'm gay."

I hadn't known, and before this incident I hadn't given

much if any thought to discrimination against gays. It's a core belief for me, and I am even more proud to have spoken out than to have found a terrific editor for *Vibe*. When you find your core beliefs, your voice needs to be loud and clear.

NAKED TRUTH #38

Forget the mission statement and all that jazz: When a company has to lay off employees, that's when its values are revealed.

As a manager, it will be your personal decisions that embody corporate values. Often you will be operating without clear company guidance. As my five-year-old would say, "Listen to your conscience."

One example is vivid. Barry Briggs, my boss at CNET, and I had just announced to the 130 employees of mySimon, a company we'd acquired a year earlier, that we would have to reduce the staff by 40 percent; almost as bad, we would be taking a week to figure out where to make the cuts, as we hadn't been close enough to the business to make those decisions without management input. (The most senior management was being fired that day.) Barry and I waited in the office of Nancy Creamer, mySimon's head of HR, for her to return from an employee meeting. A woman at least four inches shorter than my five feet three inches came to the office and asked for Nancy; I said she was out, could I take a message? She said, "Tell her 'Emily' needs to talk to her" and dissolved in wracking sobs. She was both hysterical and mortified to be crying in front of us. She finally (it seemed like an hour but was perhaps five minutes) concluded the message—it was about her visa.

Now, many people believe, and the law states, that H1-B visa holders should be the first to lose their jobs in a layoff. Jobs should be for American citizens. However, when you lay off a visa holder, they are less likely to find another job because of the costs associated with hiring them, so the chances are that they will be deported.

Barry and I knew the logical arguments. But we were not about to send Emily back to a place that so terrified her (Vietnam, as we later learned). So we waited until the head of technology made his layoff list, which turned out to include Emily, and then told him he could cut one fewer head, as long as it was she. We found the money elsewhere (that's the complicated part; someone else got added to the list). And another complicated part: If an employee had come to us calmly and professionally to ask for such special treatment, we would have agonized but probably not given it. (That's one reason that office mentions of your alternative sources of income might up the odds that you are the one laid off.)

Layoffs always involve terrible choices: Which of the employees you know are on the brink financially, with a pregnant spouse or an already laid-off partner, or who have just purchased a house, should it be. I've even watched managers wrestle with knowledge, or even suspicions, that an employee has a serious illness. Legally, none of these things should make a difference; they often do (and should).

Try to follow the laws and your company's policies if you have to make layoff decisions. But above all, listen to your conscience. When it tells you to do something different from the corporate policy, take solace in the fact that most policies are put in place to protect the company from litigation; the company probably doesn't want to know you are doing the right, rather than the stipulated, thing.

SIX

Doing the Wrong Thing— and How to Recover From a Mistake

E VERY SUCCESSFUL EXECUTIVE HAS A LONG LIST OF MIS-
takes she's made. Successful people get over their mistakes; the failures in business are the people who harp on
them or are so paralyzed by fear of mistakes that they are indecisive. Yet, perhaps because we are taught to be "good
girls," many women in business seem more tormented by
guilt over mistakes than their male counterparts. We need to
rise above that training. Almost every woman I interviewed
for this chapter, when asked to name a mistake from which
she had learned or benefited, responded, "There are so many;
let me choose one." These women achieved success on a rar-
ified level, yet commonly made mistakes, including giant
ones. So to keep you limber in mistake making, this chapter
covers my mistakes (including a giant one) and those of other
successful women, and tells how I and other mistake makers
bounced back.

If you undo a bad decision quickly, it doesn't count.

Leaving a job that has frustrations can feel wonderful until you realize you've traded a set of problems for a set of worse problems. At that point, don't let the self-doubt created by a bad decision cause you to stick with it.

When the job for which I had moved to California (at *Runner's World*) proved to be with a debasing and demoralizing company, I answered my first and last help-wanted ad and took a romantic-sounding job as marketing director of a small, profitable weekly magazine covering the Northern California arts scene. I thought I would learn a lot about art—which I love, but about which I know nothing. I quit after six weeks when the owner insisted on reading my mail and listening in on my phone calls "to see if [I was] doing a good job."

Although I had financial problems for the first time since graduating from college four years earlier, the speed of my realization meant that the job never had to appear on my résumé. Even more important, I didn't suffer from self-doubt about plunging myself into penury and giving up a high-visibility, highly paid position for one that was such a dud. This resilience comes naturally to me, but you can learn it. Absorb whatever lesson the mistake has to offer, then resolutely move on. If you fake self-confidence, eventually you will feel it.

**When you've made a mistake you are most vulnerable
to making a second in your eagerness to recover.**

In 1979 in California, unlike in my home state of New York, supermarkets accepted credit cards, so I was able to eat as I looked for another job. It was one of the many reasons I loved San Francisco and wouldn't consider returning to New York, even though employment opportunities in magazine publishing were so limited in the Bay Area. My mother helpfully reminded me, as she had annually since I finished college, that my law board scores were still valid.

After three months of unemployment, I was receptive when the publisher of *Darkroom Photography* and *Super8 Filmmaker* (which had offices just blocks from my apartment) interviewed me for the position of circulation director. My desperation almost won out, but alarm bells rang during the interview process, perhaps because the publisher talked more than he listened to my answers, and the office environment was similar to the charmless sweatshop of *Runner's World*. For once I listened to my gut, and kept living on my credit card.

Obviously, you are at your most vulnerable when trying to recover from a failed job move. But unless the wolf is truly at the door (and I don't mean giving up Starbucks for a week), be extra cautious: Taking another wrong job in haste will give you lots more time to repent at leisure. Without the lattes.

Don't ignore your growing recognition of a mistake just because you can't do anything about it . . . yet.

It's one thing to delay acting to correct a mistake—sometimes that is strategically appropriate. But don't confuse inaction with indecision. You need to recognize the mistake and plan for the best time to fix it.

When I had just assembled the team to launch *Parenting,* and we were in a frenzied four-month race to complete the debut issue, warning signs about my choice of editor quickly appeared. When editor Owen Edwards chose his number two, whom I had happened to have met months earlier through a mutual friend, I responded with delight. I had already met the man, had liked him, and was thrilled at the serendipity. Owen's uneasy silence told me that he would have preferred an executive editor with no connection to me. Because I hadn't been involved in Owen's first key hire, it set a pattern that I wasn't a part of his other key hires—and I should have been. But just because I missed the first decision, I still could have done a mid-course correction. I should have listened to my gut and insisted on access to the other top editors and the art director. Instead, I obeyed Owen's edict that I was not to talk to any of his staffers; I thought this was a way to keep everyone focused on the tasks at hand. Whenever I expressed any misgivings about editorial direction, Owen would assure me that if I were a parent, I would understand that he was doing all the right things.

If I had stood my ground, I might have learned that his staff agreed with my concerns about his direction, he might have moved to an acceptable middle ground, and I might not have had to fire him soon after the launch.

My mistake here was not to own the power I had. That sounds kind of New Age-y, but I've seen it in other women. For the first time in my career I could control every aspect of the magazine. I didn't step up to that responsibility. When you go into a new job with new levels of authority, you should think about every area and make a conscious decision: Is the management doing a good job? Inertia is never a good state.

NAKED TRUTH #42

Do not let your shame or embarrassment over a huge mistake lead you to an even bigger one: accepting others' punishment. Just because you screwed up doesn't mean you aren't the best person for the job.

Mainly because I didn't exert enough control over the editorial content in *Parenting*'s first issue, the magazine missed crucial performance benchmarks stipulated in my contract with Time Inc. The consequences were draconian: Time had no obligation to continue funding the start-up. I thought that a shutdown was unlikely, because of the advertising success of the launch, but I thought it highly likely that Reg Brack, the new Time Inc. CEO, who had not been in power when my deal was done, would replace me—as was his right. In fact, that was an automatic result of the failure; I had to convince Reg to ignore the provisions of the contract, not an easy thing for an officer of a public corporation to do. Additionally, Reg had divested the company of at least one of his predecessor's acquisitions, at a fire-sale price. I had no reason to believe I wouldn't join that heap.

Instead of berating myself over my poor performance, I buoyed myself for the showdown with Reg by rereading our positive press and advertising results and promises for future issues, and by knowing our numbers cold. I made my case: I could do the best job of running the magazine, as long as I wasn't demotivated by having ownership taken away from me; the benchmarks didn't take into account that we were a great advertising success, and firing the founder might raise enough questions to threaten that success; and we could adjust the buyout formula to repay Time for the extra money that the mistake in editorial direction had cost. I had a revised plan that included replacing Owen as editor and some educated guesses about how reader response rates might improve with better editorial.

To my astonishment and delight, Reg agreed that removing me would be a bad idea. He told me that the conversation would have been different if our shortfall had been in advertising, because the financial impact would be more difficult to calculate. As long as Time Inc.'s economics were unchanged (that is, the extra investment would come from my pocket at the time of a buyout), he would agree to ignore Time's contractual right to oust me and take most of my equity.

You are probably your toughest critic when you've made a giant mistake. Don't add to your punishment. Focus on what you've done right, and on how much you learned from the mistake. When you need to defend your record, find your sweet spot for confidence building.

When I sold my interest in *Parenting* to Time I was named a vice president of magazine development; I oversaw launches such as *Vibe* and *Martha Stewart Living* while still running *Parenting*. Perhaps success went to my head, because I then made the worst mistake of my career so far: accepting a "promotion" to run a company in which I had almost no interest, for which I had almost no affinity, and which necessitated a spirit-breaking commute and my removal from the start-up activities on which I thrived. In hopes that you will never do something as dumb, here's where I erred, and what I learned.

At the time I sold my interest in *Parenting* to Time, they had just purchased Sunset Publishing. I was not considered as a potential CEO for it, which made sense and hurt my feelings simultaneously.

The CEO they hired for Sunset never fit into the Time Inc. mold, at least not the mold of the nineties. I had tried to welcome him to the fold by inviting him to lunch soon after he started; he brought his vice president of corporate communications with him. When a group of California publishers became active in the ultimately successful effort to overturn a sales tax that discriminated against publishers based in our state, I tried to get his interest, as Sunset was the iconic California magazine; he sent the same vice president. Despite our lack of rapport, I empathized: He had a tough job. Not unlike attending an ex-boyfriend's wedding, I was still piqued at the fact that I hadn't been considered for the position, but it sure didn't look like fun. Time Inc. had paid dearly for Sunset, which had been run—as many family businesses are—at a breakeven, with the Lane family keeping on many long-service employees at a staffing level about double what comparable publishing companies had. At the time of the acquisition, Time offered lavish retirement packages to those who volunteered for them, with the result that many of the people who remained with the company did so because they had no other employment opportunities or were comfortable in their routines. Many of those who left did so because they could pocket the package and go on to something else. This is not a recipe for a vibrant staff. Moreover, California was in a fairly severe recession, so much of what Sunset had been built on—the leading edge of Western consumption, the fast growth of the California economy—was missing, at least temporarily.

My last encounter with Sunset's CEO was perhaps the oddest. We had a Time Inc. Ventures (TIV) meeting in L.A., and for the first time, TIV CEO Bob Miller—boss of both the Sunset CEO and me—decided to bring his glamorous wife, Kelly Harmon, to dinner. We met at Spago, and she was as stunning in person as on television. As we waited for our cars after dinner Kelly said to me, "Robin, I am sorry we didn't get to sit near each other. Bob tells me you are the most honest person he knows." It was flattering and refreshing to talk with a nonbusiness type. As soon as she left the Sunset CEO said bitterly, "What are the rest of us, chopped liver?" The rest of us were silent.

The handwriting was on the wall that Sunset would soon have a new CEO. Without giving it much thought, I said to Bob, "You know, if you make a change at Sunset, this time I'd like to talk about it." He said, "I'm making a change on Monday. Start talking." I didn't spend too much time thinking about what would prove to be my worst career decision. And I spent no time thinking about the content of the job—that should have been a warning signal. I chose the boyfriend who looked good on paper and who fed my ego, not the one who made my heart sing.

NAKED TRUTH #44

Doing a simple list of pros/cons before making a life-changing decision may help you recognize the true message from your gut when ego is muffling it. At least it buys time, which may allow your head to clear.

If I had done a list about becoming CEO of Sunset, it might have looked like this:

The positives:

- bigger company to run
- higher visibility (on the West Coast, Sunset is a revered institution)
- change
- public recognition that *Parenting* was not the only notch in my belt

The negatives:

- over two hours commuting daily for a newlywed planning her first pregnancy
- expectation that the CEO would make the too-high purchase price Time had paid for the company look justified
- lack of interest in gardening, food, and home improvement (most of what the magazine covered)

If I had made that list, perhaps I would have realized that even the "positives" were external and not what made me happy.

My best friend, Peggy, came to San Francisco; we'd skipped our traditional birthday trip in May, as it had just been a few months since my wedding, but now we spent time shopping for clothes for my new life (Menlo Park being warmer than San Francisco, and Sunset then being much more formal than *Parenting*), then heading to the Sonoma Mission Inn. I wanted to be relaxed, massaged, and facialed for my Sunset debut. On our final day, she was at the pool when I went into the locker room and bent down, gashing my forehead on an open locker. I have lived in California long enough that I should have recognized an omen when it literally hit me in the face. Again, I missed the warning sign that this Sunset job was not going to be right for me.

I met Bob at the airport the next day for breakfast. The plan was for him to precede me in Menlo Park, announce the choice to the executive team, address any concerns, and then I would arrive. For the first time, Bob told me that Don Logan and Reg Brack (Time Inc.'s CEO and chairman, respectively) had opposed his choice of me to run Sunset. I was shocked, but the full impact didn't hit me until later. I asked why. Bob sloughed it off, saying that they thought the new head should be an advertising type, or at least Bob should install me with an advertising sales–type at my side, since that was where Sunset's troubles mainly lay. I was hurt by Don and Reg's lack of support. Instead, I should have seen it objectively: when top management opposes your boss promoting you, you've got a problem even if you get the promotion. It should have been on my list as a giant negative.

Men seem to be more decisive than women. And, frankly, more driven by ego concerns in their decision making. Although in general I wouldn't want to slow down women's already too slow decision making, if you are quickly making a momentous decision, slowing down a bit to make sure it's not ego-driven is time well spent.

NAKED TRUTH #45

Women are damned as aggressive If we negotiate for more pay, and damnably underpaid If we don't.
Force yourself to negotiate, and learn how.

Then Bob told me what my raise would be: a mere $25,000 in my base salary (about 10 percent, or less than enough to pay for the commute costs), although my bonus would increase to a 75 percent target. I was disappointed, but quickly forgot that in the excitement of the day. Needless to say, I didn't try to negotiate my pay. I have never done that, and it is one of just two regrets I have about my career. I know for a fact that I was paid less than equivalent male executives during my Time Inc. career, and attribute the difference not to conscious discrimination, but to my typically female lack of aggressiveness about compensation. I have always earned more money than I needed, but I think I let other women down by my wimpiness.

I am not alone. A recent study of the starting salaries of people who graduated with master's degrees from Carnegie Mellon University showed that men earned nearly $4,000 per year more than women with similar majors; 57 percent of the men didn't automatically accept the starting salary offered for their first job; only 7 percent of the women negotiated for more. Those gaps widen over time from the starting job, too. Professor Linda Babcock, who conducted the study, co-authored a book *Women Don't Ask: Negotiation and the Gender Divide*. I guarantee you I will read it before taking another job.

Jan Brandt has always been terrific about negotiating her compensation. She is not shy about using drama to make her point, and refuses to be held down by whatever level her previous job may have been. "The first person to talk loses, so when they ask, how much do you want to make or what is your current salary, you don't respond. When you *have* to say something, say, 'I'm receptive to an offer. What is the range?' Don't bring it up first. Frequently they will give a bigger number than you expected." And for her final parry, when she and the man hiring her were twenty-five thousand dollars apart on a number, she told him, "'I can't do this. I can do great things for your company. It would be a shame to blow that for a small amount. How about this: When you go to sleep tonight, think about what I'm worth. If when you wake up you are thinking about me, you need to call me and pay me what I want.' He did."

Follow Jan's example instead of mine, and you will retire richer. She travels on a private plane.

As I waited for the appointed time to show up at Sunset, I grew more apprehensive. I'd been comparing myself to my predecessor, and that felt like an easy act to follow. But the physical reality of showing up at Sunset's legendary head-quarters made me queasy. There were four buildings (one sublet and one vacant; the other two housed the book and magazine properties separately) and vast, renowned gardens originally designed by Thomas Church. The main building was designed by Clifford May, one of the preeminent Califor-nia ranch-house architects, and it felt like a private estate. There was a large patio for entertaining, with a giant fire-place, glass doors that could be opened to the gardens in warm weather (just about all the time in Menlo Park), a com-pany wine cellar, and kitchens. I felt like a pretender to a for-eign crown.

I killed some time getting my Toyota washed, then swung into the circular driveway. I knew that my predecessor had insisted on parking his Jag there—employees parked in a lot around the corner—and was resolved not to follow his ex-ample, but I had no other way in at that point.

My appointment stunned many at Sunset. (I was later

told that the longtime art director exclaimed, "They think a girl can run this place?") I was probably the most stunned. At *Parenting*, I was supremely comfortable with the atmosphere I had created, and was surrounded by fellow San Franciscans of similar ages and appearance to me. At Sunset, almost one hundred years had created an atmosphere ("the adobe womb") unlike any workplace I'd seen, and the employees wore suits and dresses (incongruously, for the offices looked like a gracious home). At *Parenting*, my office was open and in the center of the action. At Sunset, my assistant had her own office outside my giant one, so people had to run a gauntlet just to see if I was in. At first I scorned my private bathroom—I had found ladies' room chats one of my best sources of information in past jobs—but soon gave in to the convenience. And the publicity surrounding my appointment made it easy to ignore my unease: The *New York Times* called me a "corporate entrepreneur," and I liked to think of the various people who'd thought I was a one-trick pony forced to admit that Time thought otherwise. That part, if not the reality of the job, was heady.

How can you distinguish between the headiness of a move made for ego reasons and the excitement of a new job that you've taken for the right reasons? If the preponderance of the excitement rests on things like your office, your pay, the announcement, your friends' (or rivals') or parents' reactions . . . watch out. Those can exist, but hopefully in balance with things like the joy of discovering exciting new colleagues, rising to an impossible challenge, and anticipating rolling up your sleeves and getting something done.

THE BEST MISTAKES OF
SUCCESSFUL WOMEN

The women I interviewed had a common response to the question: "Tell me about a mistake you made, and what you learned." Almost to a woman, they answered, "There were so many, how can I choose?" Some ultimately chose one-time mistakes that changed the way they led their businesses or lives. Others ruefully pointed out a mistake they made over and over, in hopes that other women could avoid it. But most of these "mistakes" benefited the women in their later choices, and all offer lessons for others.

I held on too long. Most of the women felt they had delayed a tough move—particularly in the area of firing—longer than they should have. Dianne Snedaker spoke for many: "Mistakes were all about not making hard decisions about people earlier. It's just like personal relationships: Sometimes you hang in wanting to believe you can change things, but you need to know when to leave, when it's crossed a line to [such] a point [that] you are being compromised." Karen Behnke was blunt: "As soon as you suspect it's not going to work out, fire the person. It's better for you, for them, for the business."

Mary Ann Byrnes, who as CEO took wireless company Corsair public, says she has stayed too long in the wrong job: "When things start going wrong for reasons outside of my control, I feel I can't be viewed as a quitter; I don't want to be credited with the problem [and] have to stay until it's fixed."

This hanging-on-too-long applies to other business decisions: Marion McGovern was shocked by a landlord's claim that they were owed $380,000 and ongoing revenues because of a technical clause in her lease triggered by the sale of her business. Her company incurred over $1 million in legal fees and severe business disruption (being served with eviction notices and endless court filings) before she decided to settle the suit: "I was right on principle, but I should have settled earlier. Litigation takes on a life of its own. I still feel terrible about settling."

I didn't get paid enough. Others echo my own regrets about my failure to negotiate compensation packages. Hilary Schneider ruefully comments, "I've got the Imposter Syndrome—really can't believe anyone would want to hire me, so of course I don't feel underpaid. I don't negotiate." Jan Brandt, vice chair emeritus and former chief marketing officer of AOL, is probably the most financially successful of the women I interviewed. Not coincidentally, she was the least shy about tough compensation negotiations. "My answer to that is to lie. I have lied about money almost every time I was hired. They were trying to pay me seventy cents on the dollar, being the female, and that was how I compensated and the only way I could get paid what I deserved."

I went into a dying business. Business failures were often cited as the best learning experiences. Hilary Schneider says, "I went to Red Herring [a now-defunct New Economy publication] during the Internet heyday. I'd been at Times Mirror for ten years, but the company was purchased and they wanted me to move to Chicago. So I took the Red Herring job, and for eighteen months of incredible stress managed a declining business. We couldn't adjust quickly enough to realities. I learned more about leadership than in the rest of my career added together. How to recruit, motivate, make decisions during a downward spiral. No one looking at my résumé will recognize it as anything but a misstep, but I'm a better executive for doing that job." Valli Benesch took over her family's apparel business and promptly opened a division: "Disaster. So badly received. I had to close it immediately. It was very humiliating. But I knew we had to change our image with department stores, and the failure taught me that we needed to do it gradually. I transformed existing divisions gradually, then added new ones that could use the current product as a springboard."

I should have gotten a haircut. Carol Smith, senior vice president/ELLE Group publishing director, commented, "I've made this mistake a million times. I got a little bored and frustrated in my job, and someone offered me another one, and I jumped into the wrong one. It's like the Woody Allen thing: 'You want *me?* Damn, I must be good.' I should have gone shopping or gotten my hair cut instead."

I burnt a bridge. Nancy O'Neill, a former Times Mirror corporate officer and president of several operating units, had a summer job at *USA Today* while enrolled at Harvard Business School: "I was very underutilized, because they didn't have other MBAs. I was dissatisfied with the summer experience, but when they made a full-time offer for me post graduation, I told her way more than she asked. I should have kept my dissatisfaction to myself or vented to a friend. It didn't serve any purpose."

I chose the wrong partner. When she started Gardener's Eden catalog, Ruth Owades knew that the investor group she'd found would be difficult: "They tried to micromanage everything I did. The first catalog did okay, not great. My gut was to test a Christmas catalog, despite the fact that gardening is more in the spring/summer. My investors were dead set against it." The only way she could get free to do the mailing was to issue an ultimatum to her partners: "'Either buy me out at fifty cents on the dollar or I buy you out.' I knew that they loved telling me what to do but wouldn't want to actually do the work themselves." That Christmas mailing saved her business.

Sue Marks, the founder and former CEO of Pro Staff, an independent staffing company in Wisconsin that she sold to Kelly Services, started her business at twenty-four. Because she and her initial partner were incompatible, she "mortgaged my house and borrowed money from my family to buy him out." The buyout coincided with the birth of her first child.

I gave an ultimatum and wasn't ready to follow through. The women differed on whether you should ever do this, but agreed that if you give one, be prepared to execute it. Jan Brandt: "*Never* give anyone an ultimatum. I did it once. 'Unless you promote me, I'm quitting.' The next day I apologized. And started sending out résumés."

I assumed friendship would make a difference. Beth Sawi, former chief administrative officer of Charles Schwab, comments, "You shouldn't assume that because you and your boss are friendly that he really likes you, that he will be willing to take risks about giving you a new opportunity. I had a very positive working relationship with my boss, but when a sales position became available, he wouldn't overlook my lack of direct experience and give me a chance."

I took the wrong job. This was a common mistake, particularly early in their careers, but never fatal. Carol Smith chose between an early job in corporate lending at Citibank and one as the first woman in ad sales at the *Wall Street Journal*. "I took the Citi job because it was amazing to be offered it since I didn't have an MBA. I was there seven days and went to the lobby to call the *Journal* and see if they still wanted me. That's how I started in media." Nancy O'Neill thought that her Harvard MBA meant she was ready for senior management, so she declined a classic marketing position at Procter & Gamble because "it sounded too junior. I couldn't stand the thought of having to prove myself. So I had to teach myself on the job and in my free time, which was much harder and took longer." In Jan Brandt's case, the mistake was starting her own company. "First, I picked an area I did well in but wasn't passionate about. Second, I don't think I like being the first one in—I like a little structure and momentum already there."

Sometimes, an apparently wrong job choice works out just fine. Ginger Graham was at Eli Lilly. "They asked me to do something no other director would have found appropriate: I ended up writing speeches for the CEO. He was the president of the Pharmaceutical Manufacturers Association. He gave me hours at his desk, answering my questions. He'd been leading the industry for longer than I'd been out of diapers. It was a gift rather than something I was stuck with."

You will make mistakes. Resilience will rescue you. Women tend to be much more self-critical and perfectionist than men, which can make mistakes more painful. Leslie Jacobs, former CEO of the Rosenthal Agency, one of the top one hundred insurance brokers in the United States, had a great technique for disaster recovery: "I allow myself two days of self-pity and flagellation, and then it's time to move on. I am a deadline type of person. I put it on the calendar. Two days."

SEVEN

Hiring Stars— and Keeping Them

I AM GOOD AT PICKING PEOPLE WHO WILL CONTRIBUTE TO the organization. It's a reason why other managers often ask me to interview candidates even when the position doesn't directly involve me. While I don't do much screening for technical or specific expertise, I do look for an appropriate psychological profile, value system, and cultural fit. Here are some ways I find the keepers:

Get a Candid Answer

I have a canned question I ask of all candidates: "Hiring people is the hardest thing we do. Please give me a specific example—granular, a specific individual, although I don't need a name—of a person with whom you succeeded as a manager in adding value to their development or to the company's results. Then give me an example, again a specific one, of a person with whom you failed as a manager, and what you learned." I have found this question spectacular in learning what people are really like, which is more important than their philosophies of management. Here are some exchanges with candidates I didn't hire:

Male Interviewee: "I believe in nurturing my people's strengths and discussing any development needs with them."
"Can you give me a specific example of a person and how you nurtured strengths or discussed development needs?"
"I was promoted to vice president because I am such a good manager."

Another man: "A woman who worked for me is now a vice president in another department of the company."
"That's great. How did you help her grow when she was in your department?"
"She was a star, she didn't really need anything from me."
"Is there an example of someone who wasn't such a star who did need some guidance from you?"
"I've forgotten about the bad performers."

Some choose examples that reveal themselves as micromanagers, or otherwise limited. ("I had an engineer who never came in on time. That could be okay in a tech company, but we were a bank and needed set hours. I documented this—we had to do everything by the book with HR—and finally fired him and got someone better.") Some are incapable of discussing specific examples, and get caught in generalities polished by lots of interviewing. (Citing management theory books is an immediate tip-off.) Many have begun with a canned success story and forgotten the second half of the question (lack of attention to detail in an interview is not a good thing).

I prefer the candidates who start with the failures; many have commented, "I need to start with a story that has bothered me for years." I like the candor, the reflection of a sincere concern for people, and the demonstration of a willingness to learn from mistakes. I should commemorate a candidate for a COO position. This man, who had managed hundreds of people, responded after much thought that he had never had a failure. I pressed him, and he insisted that his batting average as a manager was perfect. I eliminated him for either a great lie, or great self-delusion. Perhaps he was the one perfect manager, but the odds were against it.

Another terrific question is: "Tell me who would give you the most glowing review, who would give you the worst, and who would give an accurate appraisal. Then tell me what each would say."

Get to the Tricky Stuff Carefully, But Get to It

Another well-qualified candidate for a catalog company included a reference to his religious faith on his résumé. This was so unusual that it was a red flag for me—but asking about religion is a quick way to get sued. Instead, after a long phone interview, I asked him if he'd thought about the differences involved in managing a Bay Area company, with its more diverse workforce than he was used to in the Midwest. He said all the correct and unrevealing things. I then commented, "I've been surprised by how much cursing the employees do." He responded by saying how uncomfortable that would make him, and that he would forbid it. We didn't bother bringing him to the Bay Area for an interview, although I had a great restaurant with cross-dressing waiters in mind if we did. While being religious and socially conservative would be appropriate for many companies, it could be a fatal limitation on managing talent in the Bay Area.

Get Another Opinion

I love to interview in tandem with a colleague. I don't know why this is not more common, as even a mediocre interviewing partner will give you more insight into a prospective candidate. When I've suggested it to colleagues they sometimes worry that it would intimidate candidates, but my view is that if the candidate is shaken by interviewing with two people at once, you need to consider whether he has the chutzpah to succeed in the job.

Get the Real Story

Most people stink at checking references. (In fact, very few references are checked unless a headhunter is handling the search, and most headhunters are looking for good news, not bad.) The résumé and references don't matter if my gut tells me not to hire someone. However, if my gut tells me someone is right for the job, I still check references. Salespeople in particular can create that good "gut feeling" even if they are absolutely the wrong choice for the position. I have a rule: The less I want to check references—because my chemistry is great with the candidate or I am desperate to fill the position—the more I force myself to follow up on every lead.

Now, I will admit that checking references has become

more difficult because of litigation—most companies absolutely forbid employees from giving references. However, there are ways around the problem. I believe in a favor bank, which means that I try to do whatever is in my power to help people I know. That way, when I need information about a prospective employee, the chances are that if they've worked in media, or at an Internet company, I know someone who owes me a favor who will talk off the record. Needless to say, I don't stop at the names provided by the candidate. I look for holes—past supervisors who aren't listed, for example—and for contacts with whom I can get down and dirty.

Checking references is not the whole solution, however. You need to ferret out the bad news from someone determined not to give it to you. The best technique is long silences, because the interviewee will often talk to fill them. Listening much more than talking during an interview sounds obvious, but is often violated.

NAKED TRUTH #47

Help (with reference or referral) almost anyone who asks for it in their job search; explain reason if declining.

NAKED TRUTH #48

Never help someone a second time if they didn't report back the results of the first reference.

Perhaps this advice should be in the chapter on manners, but it bears repeating. Everyone I know who is in a position to give significant references on people who've worked for her says the same thing: The candidate who lets you know the outcome of a job search is the exception.

I recently gave a reference for a former colleague about whom I have very mixed feelings; the headhunter doing the search had heard of me and insisted on contacting me, though I wasn't listed as a reference. The former colleague then had a mutual friend ask for my help and I agreed, since the job would play to her strengths instead of her weaknesses. I never heard anything from the former colleague, who knew she wouldn't have gotten the job without my reference. I hope she stays employed there forever, because I won't be available next time.

Perhaps I sound too sensitive, too easily affronted. But the candidate's failure to thank me was a reminder that her people skills were nonexistent; she didn't credit her staff or communicate easily. Clearly the decade since we'd worked together hadn't taught her much about communication.

NAKED TRUTH #49

Your most valuable asset is the favor bank. Help others and they will help you.

Talking candidly also helps in finding the right candidate. When you establish yourself as someone who will tell the truth, others return the favor.

When I was overseeing the test of *Vibe* we had a short

timeframe to find someone who knew the music and had the editorial talent to edit it. Ideally, the candidate would have been a black man, reflecting the core audience. I called Adam Moss (now the editor-in-chief of *New York* magazine), a great judge of talent, and he responded with a candidate who was both white and gay. Adam was a good enough friend that I could express my reservations on that score without fear of lawsuit, but Adam assured me that "he loves that music—in his heart he's a fourteen-year-old black girl."

If you don't have a long enough work history to have built up a favor bank, reach out to others who can identify candidates or check references. Tell the source that you are new to your position, or to your company, and that making a bad hiring decision might end your career/job/life. Assure them that whatever they say will be kept in total confidence. If you are still getting pablum, invent a plausible concern about the candidate—"I really like Sam but am worried that he might be overly detail-oriented instead of understanding the big picture"—and see if you can spark a defense.

Get Going

Timing is everything. A candidate who might turn you down on Monday might be having a bad day on Tuesday. Keep calling. Valli Benesch, former chairman and the CEO of the apparel company Fritzi California, says, "I wanted to recruit a star; she was number two at one of our competitors. She said no, but I didn't give up. I would call her two, three times a week for six months. I just kept checking in. I knew she could be great. I finally hit her at a weak moment, and she stayed with us twenty years."

Get a Contract

This tip is for when you are being hired. (If you are doing the hiring, try to resist giving a contract.) Contracts set the minimum package for when you are fired, and your leverage is always greatest before you step into a job. Timing is key here: Work out the important details (salary, bonus) first, then get it in writing. If the response to your request for a contract is that it is against company policy, ask if any exceptions have ever been made. (There are always exceptions.) When all the standard arguments for why you need a contract fail to convince, pull the emotion card: You will work better in the job if you don't have to worry about feeding your family while out of work. Even if you fail to get a contract—you are being hired by a company that really really never gives contracts at your level—you will learn a lot from your potential boss's responses about the environment you will be entering. If she is reasonable and convincing, you can feel good even if you don't have a contract. If she gets offended or defensive, don't say I didn't warn you.

NAKED TRUTH #50

Given one candidate with perfect qualifications and one for whom the position would be a stretch, if the latter seems more excited about the opportunity, choose him/her.

It amazes me how people who should know better fail to consider the candidate's motivations in wanting the job. The motivation of the candidate trumps her qualifications, at least for most jobs. This often means hiring someone who has never had that level of responsibility before rather than the person who's got all the requisite experience and nothing left to prove.

Dianne Snedaker comments, "You can learn a skill, but you need to start with enthusiasm, excitement, curiosity. Too much of work takes the attitude out of us. You have to start with a great attitude." One of the best receptionists I ever hired was at *Mother Jones,* and I found her through a state employment program for recovering addicts. "Eleanor" was from a well-to-do family, but her heroin habit had led to a résumé that mainly featured exotic dancing. Okay, stripping. Eleanor explained that a structured job like we were offering would help her stay straight, and I decided that it didn't take much experience to be a good receptionist. The consequences for Eleanor if she failed in the job were surely greater than for most of the other applicants, so I decided to take the chance. She was grateful for the chance to prove herself, and was a terrific receptionist and delightful presence in the office.

Despite that example, don't mistake a candidate who needs a job for one who wants it. Your responsibility is to employ the right person, not the neediest one.

NAKED TRUTH #51

Resist the temptation to "sell" prospective team members. Your key managers need to sell themselves, or they won't be there for the long haul.

My first choice for editor of *Parenting* opted out. Jeffrey Klein, my favorite *Mother Jones* colleague, worked on the direct-mail test for *Parenting*, but then told me, "I should be thinking of ideas for this magazine when I'm in the shower. If I were the right editor, I would be." I was lucky that he took his own temperature; I was so desperate to field a team that I overlooked his lack of enthusiasm.

Once you have hired the stars, here's one little tip which I hope will help you as much as it did me: Give gifts. I don't mean the typical Christmas or major-milestone recognition. I mean something unexpected, for no reason except to show appreciation. It doesn't have to be expensive, but it has to be from the heart.

A year or two after I'd sold *Parenting* to Time Inc. I almost lost Carol, my partner (and eventual successor). The Calyx & Corolla catalog had introduced the concept, now common, of "A Year of Flowers." I always paid the catalog extra attention because a friend founded it, and decided to send Carol a year of flowers—it cost around four hundred dollars (and of course I didn't put things like that on my expense account). My timing turned out to be perfect. She was being lured by KIII to be president of *Seventeen*, at a compensation package that would have doubled what she was making at *Parenting*. To add to the allure of the job, Carol and I had tried, and failed, to convince Time to acquire *Sassy* as a rival to *Seventeen*, so this job would have been sweet revenge. I did get permission from Don Logan to exceed Time's usual limit of a 25 percent bump in compensation in a given year, to come close to meeting KIII's package, but the flowers made the difference. Carol told me that she hadn't planned to ask for a counteroffer before she got the flowers, which reminded her of the importance of our relationship in her ability to do her job.

SECRETS OF SUCCESSFUL TEAMS

Parenting launched at roughly the same time, with roughly the same mission, as two other magazines: *Child* and *Children*. Today there is no doubt who won the race: *Children* is long defunct, and *Child* is a fraction of the size of *Parenting*. As any venture capitalist would tell you, the one critical success factor is the management team. Here are the most important points in selecting and empowering that team:

- **Across-team communication.** An accepted business theory is that teams that worked together previously do better the second time around than do newly assembled teams. I had only worked with two of my four top managers, but the other two had worked together previously. And Carol, my most important partner, and I established a trust and an open communication pattern at our first meeting that continues today.
- **Freedom from fear.** Business can be terrifying. If your managers are afraid to bring you bad news, you might as well fold up the tent.
- **Share your thought process.** There is no room for an imperial presence in most companies, but particularly not in small ones. Carol was not thrilled with my choice of Owen as editor (she was right); my circulation director and general manager disliked each other intensely (their mutual criticisms were valid, but they both did good jobs). In each case I shared my reasoning for selecting the members of the team, and got their cooperation and mainly good behavior as a result. Even when I made the wrong decision the team held together because they were heard and understood my reasoning.

You'll notice that "loyalty" is not a trait I put on the list. While clearly you can't have a team member who is treacherous, many leaders mistake blind obedience for loyalty. Former treasury secretary (and successful CEO) Paul O'Neill, in Ron Suskind's brilliant *The Price of Loyalty*, put it well: "That's a false kind of loyalty, loyalty to a person and whatever they say or do, that's the opposite of real loyalty, which is loyalty based on inquiry, and telling someone what you really think and feel—your best estimation of the truth instead of what they want to hear."

Start-ups have a particular challenge in putting together the team in that sometimes the risk level is just too high for someone perfectly qualified. Timing is everything. The key is to prioritize the must-have characteristics of team members, because even in an established company you may not be able to get exactly what you are looking for. In the key hires I made for *Parenting* each had a major gap in his or her résumé that I chose to overlook because of other attributes:

KEY HIRE	PLUS	MINUS
Carol Smith, Publisher	Two lean-budget magazine launches	Almost no experience in most of *Parenting*'s major advertising categories
Owen Edwards, Editor	Terrific speaker and writer	Little management experience; most of career spent as a freelance writer
Fran Reilly, Circulation Director	Demonstrated success managing circulation on a razor-thin budget	Lack of formal training or education meant limited presentation skills

In retrospect I can say that Carol and Fran's minuses could be—and were—overcome with experience; Owen's was a fatal flaw because it reflected a fundamental choice in his way of working (alone).

· Finally, while I think a variety of types can get a company off the ground, building a successful business is different, and it requires a CEO, not just a leader/founder. CEOs fall into two camps: One chooses people better—more expert, more driven, more talented or more of a specialist—than they are; the other chooses those to whom they feel superior. The former are more rare, and will be more successful. Which would you prefer to be, or to work for?

EIGHT

Firing . . .
From Both Sides

I HAVE FIRED A LOT OF PEOPLE. COUNTING LAYOFFS, WHICH are somewhat less personal than performance-based firings, the number is in the hundreds. But regardless of the overall total, I have certainly had to dismiss dozens in the up-close-and-personal category, where I have had to look someone in the eye and tell him he has to leave the company. Even with all this previous experience I don't breathe any easier before I fire someone—I still have a pounding heart and a sleepless night beforehand. However, the aftermath is definitely easier on me. I hope the same is true for the person I've fired.

NAKED TRUTH #52

If you've had management responsibility and have never fired anyone, you probably should be a candidate for the ax. It comes with the territory.

Part of how I came to terms with this always tough process is by learning that most of the people I have fired have ended up in jobs better suited to them; if they are not making more money, then they are at least being successful in their new jobs instead of struggling as in their former ones. I have never fired someone and later regretted it: The replacements were always better. I do have regrets—often—that I failed as the manager to turn around a performance problem. But by the time I pull the trigger I have come to grips with my own failure, and then with the employee's. And in every case I probably should have fired the person sooner than I did.

My initiation into firing was cut-and-dried: My first assistant stole the driver's license of a coworker so that she could drink in a bar. Few cases since that first one have been so simple. I have fired people who haven't tried to mend their ways, but mainly they have been decent, hardworking, and nice to me (if not to their peers or staffs). While I don't count anyone I've fired among my friends (after the fact), there are few whom I would be embarrassed or afraid to meet on the street or at an industry function. It's like breaking up with a guy: try for a civil ending.

What does that mean? Bite your tongue if provoked. Don't try to have the last word (the end of his paycheck accomplishes that). You don't need to prove yourself right—you have the power. Be generous in spirit and severance.

NAKED TRUTH #53

The toughest firing decision is when you are to blame for not defining the job correctly, or for making the wrong hire, or for not jumping on the problem when it first arose.

I have agonized over many firings, but I shouldn't have. The most dramatic one was Owen Edwards, *Parenting*'s founding editor. I had allowed him to keep me at a distance from the editorial product of the magazine I had created, and I had ignored my growing uneasiness that the result was a magazine very different from my vision, and very different from what readers would want. Because I felt sheepish for having given him too much rope at the outset, I was tentative as I tried to put him on a shorter leash, and he would have none of it.

With years more experience, I can advise you to do what I didn't: get over your self-flagellation for failing to set the right working relationship from the beginning. Do what fits with your personal style: Mine is to tell the employee that I blew it at the outset and need to establish a new way of working together. You might want to be less explicit or more formal, but the point still needs to be made: Starting today, here are the new ground rules and here is what needs to change. Even if you erred on the side of not taking enough power, as I had in this instance, you don't need to worry about not getting it. You are the boss, and as soon as you start acting like one, the person will shape up or be shipped out.

NAKED TRUTH #54

Create a culture where your direct reports can voice their concerns about their peers to you, but where they understand that indirect criticism, or talking about their concerns with anyone else, will not be tolerated.

I'll return to the example of *Parenting*'s first editor because there were many elements that made it difficult for me as a manager. It was hard for me to accept that I had let such a disastrous situation occur. The magazine was a runaway success with advertisers, but readers' dissatisfaction was clear to insiders, and I was worried that firing the editor on a high-profile launch would make skittish advertisers realize there were problems with the product. So I first tried to gain the voice I had ceded earlier.

The stakes were unbelievably high: His failure to understand the targeted audience was the probable reason that *Parenting* had missed performance benchmarks that could cause Time Inc. to fire me and take control of the magazine. Yet there was no certainty: Perhaps the benchmarks would have been missed in any case. The critical reaction to the magazine from other editors was very positive. We were a high-profile launch; Time Inc. had debated whether to invest, because giving a businessperson the ability to fire the editor was forbidden under their bylaws and traditions. Yet I knew what I had to do: The other senior members of the management team—the heads of advertising and circulation—were telling me of their worries about Owen. In the end, I was saved because I had created a nonpolitical climate where my team was empowered to voice concerns to me. When push came to the shove out the door the rest of the team helped me lead the business successfully.

How do you create a culture of constructive criticism? No matter how much you say you have an open-door policy, that you manage by walking around, whatever the buzzwords, if you show even an instant of defensiveness or aversion to bad news, it will undo all the speeches. If your first reaction to bad news from a colleague is to doubt it, keep it to yourself. Just listen until you are ready to respond in an open way.

Just as you script the conversation with the person being fired, have a plan for immediate communication with the survivors: the people who reported to, and worked with, the departing person.

Although I was worried about what Owen would say and do, I was more concerned about the remaining editorial staff. Owen had kept me so far apart from them that I had no idea how many, if any, would embrace my editorial vision. I went into Owen's office, told him the news and handed him the paperwork that detailed his severance package, and gave him time to tell his staff and clean out his personal effects. It wasn't until he had left the building that I met with his number two, who I was asking to take the reins on an "acting" basis while I searched for a new editor. Once I had his support we met with the rest of the staff to answer their questions as best as we could while respecting Owen's privacy.

You might feel so relieved that the dreaded event is over that you can be seen as not taking the firing seriously or, worse, gloating. Post firing is a time for you to be very visible and somewhat somber around the office, even though there may be increased needs for private closed-door conversations. (Later, when Owen wrote an article for GQ on "How to Fire" I was gratified to recognize—among his barbs at me and the other woman who'd notably fired him, Helen Gurley

Brown—that I had actually followed the protocol he recommended. However, he called me "a drab character on her best days" and that stung—and cost me a lot in compensatory clothing purchases.)

Most survivors after a firing have the same question: What does it mean for me? Answer both indirectly and directly. Treating the departed person with dignity communicates implicitly that if this ever happens to them it will be handled fairly. That should be enough to keep them from focusing on the fear. Meeting individually with the person's direct reports reassures them that they will not be hanged along with their boss but judged on their own contributions, while you let them know what your expectations are for change. If you pretend (either overtly or with silence) that you don't want to see immediate change, it won't reassure anyone—after all, you've shown in the most dramatic way that change is necessary. Now you need to tell them what kind of change.

NAKED TRUTH #56

When you are hired to do a turnaround, don't evaluate every senior team member to decide whether to keep him. Assume you need to fire everyone, and then judiciously choose which if any to hire back.

I wish I had known this Naked Truth before taking over at Sunset Publishing. If you are at a failing company and a new leader is brought in, assume she has read this book and that your job is in jeopardy. Prove yourself, again: What you have done in the past will be almost irrelevant, since the overall effort isn't succeeding.

My first mistake at Sunset was leaving the head of advertising in place. My boss, who had overseen Sunset's CEO for a year, liked him, and I was predisposed to keep the current players until proven wrong. I should have known that all senior ad salespeople are personable, and should have questioned the advertising director's strategic thinking and management skills much more thoroughly. If I had interviewed him in the way I would interview a prospective hire, he wouldn't have been my choice. He shouldn't have gotten bonus points for being an incumbent in a failing department.

You need to enter a new company as if you are traveling to a foreign country, and look for signs of the culture. I immediately saw that Sunset was a more formal, hierarchical organization than *Parenting,* and blithely assumed that my usual "breath of fresh air" would cause people to open up. Instead, they lied or were polite. So it was months before anyone on the management team shared their doubts about the abilities of the advertising director, and a year before anyone on the sales staff did.

Learn from my mistake. I've already talked about how to create a culture of constructive criticism (or in Paul O'Neill's term, "informed inquiry"). What if you walk into a department where a different culture exists? You can't wait for people to come to you. Draw them out. Insist in individual meetings that they tell you what's wrong (otherwise you will hear only from the complainers or those with agendas). Unless you are being handed the keys to a well-running machine (which would be unique in my work experience), there are problems to uncover.

You know more than you think you do.

The words of this Naked Truth are the opening to Dr. Benjamin Spock's classic book on raising children, and although I mostly don't see being a boss as being parental, the wisdom holds here. When you manage people your role is "big picture." Hopefully, everyone who reports to you is more knowledgeable about their area than you are, but you need to have the perspective gleaned from seeing the results. ("A" for effort might have worked in grade school, but it doesn't cut it in business.) General managers are sometimes intimidated by the expertise of people they supervise. Don't be.

I knew nothing about book publishing when I came to Sunset. The head of Sunset Books was smart and could not have been nicer to me. I agonized over the change of leadership, even though the president's style—he held fifteen hours of regularly scheduled management meetings a week, for example—was clearly not working. I brought in a consultant to make recommendations about how to bring the division to a profitability it had never enjoyed, and discussed the findings with the head of the division, who as usual was charming and open but clueless as to how to effect change. Finally, when I went in to give him the bad news, he seemed relieved.

I wasted time because I thought I had to learn a business before making a change. Just because the book publishing world was new to me didn't mean that the business was new. Bloated management teams, lack of innovation, and indecision are easy to recognize; you don't need to be an expert in the field.

*   *   *

If you take over an area that is new to you, ask the head of it for a plan to fix any large problems. If you are not convinced by the plan—if it doesn't articulate why she hadn't made the fixes previously, if it doesn't articulate immediate steps to address problems, and most of all if it doesn't take responsibility for past errors—you know enough.

NAKED TRUTH #58

Fire faster. And when it's your head that is on the block, hope—and be prepared—for a faster execution.

It was inevitable that I be fired as CEO of Sunset. Bob Miller, my boss, had chosen me over the voiced objections of both the CEO and chairman of Time Inc. Then I had listened to Bob and not replaced the head of advertising upon my arrival. I got pregnant six months into the job, and as much as I hate to admit it, I got complacent. Then, two weeks before my maternity leave began, Bob gave me an additional, failing company to run. After my son's birth, I got a new boss. No one who knew both of us thought I could work successfully for Jim, and I should have bowed out at that point.

Since business books are silent on what actually happens inside the room when an executive is being fired, I tell my painful tale here so that you can imagine being in that spot, and be prepared for it. Six months into the contract, I was called to L.A., where my boss, and his boss, worked. I forget the pretext for the meeting, but it was quickly set aside: "We've decided to make a change at Sunset next year. [It was October 2.] We think you are great, but you are a round peg in a square hole. I want you to stay with Time if you want to. No need to announce this before January. I don't know what exact responsibilities you would have; we need to see what develops. The reason for the timing is that you have said you need to make a change in editor-in-chief of Sunset, and we want the new CEO to select the editor."

I couldn't believe how calmly I responded: "Well, you've made your decision. I would have liked the opportunity to respond to any problems you've had with my leadership, since any time I ask you, you say you have none. Have you chosen my successor? You're not asking my opinion, but I think it has to be Steve."

Bob said, "We've had no conversations with him. He seems the logical choice." "So when do you want to do this?" I asked. "I could leave tomorrow. I have a contract and you aren't offering me anything specific." Bob responded, "We didn't know where this conversation would go. Let's sleep on it." I volleyed, "What's to sleep on? We can resolve it this afternoon." Bob said that it would be better for everyone if we could work out a way to keep me at the company. I said, "Well, I'll say one thing. I could announce Steve as my successor on the magazine and move into a figurehead role for a transition period. I think Sunset and Steve would benefit; his reputation is as a political backstabber, so if this were seen as my choice it would help him." Bob said, "Absolutely." He then commented, "It's amazing that those would be your first thoughts, almost the first words out of your mouth." I had the parting line: "I may be a round peg, but I care about Sunset."

Men are wimps. Virtually without exception, they avoid discussing performance problems. So when they have to fire someone, they do it badly. It costs their companies more money—and the person being fired pays a higher emotional price.

My matter-of-fact responses were my way of keeping myself together, but they also had the effect of creating goodwill with Bob (that was a lost cause with Jim). Since you never know when your paths will cross again professionally, this is always the best course of action if you can afford it emotionally. I kept a stiff upper lip in the L.A. office as I saw more junior staffers—several of whom I had coached and helped in their careers—who didn't yet know the news. But when I came through the door at home, I sobbed in my husband's arms. He waited until later to make fun of the phrase I kept repeating, "But I'm unemployable."

In retrospect, I succeeded in handling my firing: Bob's guilt over Jim's behavior, and his gratitude for my unemotional response, led him to significantly enhance the money I was contractually guaranteed. He justified the additional funds by "optioning" my time for future projects, even though I knew there would be none. The Sunset staff was spared the knowledge of yet another management failure, at least until my successor spilled the beans months later. And I had several months of lame-duck status, during which time I followed my own rule for "what to do when it happens to you": Reach out to your friends and colleagues, and do it quickly. Many people will feel awkward, even if your departure is announced as a resignation. They don't know your state of mind and don't know what to say. Make it easy for them: Send a cheery letter with as much as you can about future plans, and give them your contact information. You will be amazed at the people who contact you, and the opportunities that result.

HOW TO FIRE

I follow the standard HR principles, but it's startling how few CEOs do.

- **No surprises.** I take pride in the fact that even employees with great powers of denial are not surprised when I ultimately fire them, because by that point we have had numerous conversations about the problems. Have the tough conversations. I think women are much better at this than men, perhaps because our girlfriends want feedback on their looks, choices in boyfriends, shopping decisions—once you've told a friend that perhaps cosmetic surgery is not such a bad idea, most subjects come easy. Giving tough feedback is imperative, but although people consider me brutally honest, I don't rely on my native candor. I script tough performance conversations in advance, with the points I need to make. It is way too easy to gloss over the tough truths, especially if you like the person you are supervising. You owe it to him to hit all the key points. Likewise, an annual performance review should not be the first time an employee hears of your concerns; the formality of that setting makes criticism feel even harsher. Regular conversations make it easier for an employee to absorb developmental feedback.
- **Keep it simple.** This is not the time to be delivering an analysis of the person's failures (see previous rule). He can't absorb more than the information of his firing, and if you feel a need to go into all the reasons, it's probably because you are feeling insecure. But answer his questions, as straightforwardly and simply as you can.
- **Consider the location.** I try to preserve the person's dignity to the greatest extent possible. This usually means going into the person's office; he can then collect himself in the

most comfortable setting before venturing out. (And I can choose the moment to end the conversation by leaving.)

- **Anticipate the reaction.** You can make an educated guess about the person's reaction, and be better prepared for it. (Most good HR people will role-play with you, which I have done to great results in key firings.) For example, true to stereotype, men don't usually want to engage in a discussion, or talk you out of the decision. (However, the one time I needed to fire a man I had slept with, many years earlier, I had someone else do it.)

- **Don't chicken out.** I've heard of people changing their minds about firing someone midconversation. I've never heard of one of those situations turning out well.

- **Keep your cool.** I think twice before firing anyone I am angry at, and have usually reached equanimity before pulling the trigger. Several people I have fired have asked me to serve as a reference, and I have been happy to do so. (I stress the positive and don't lie when pressed. Few interviewers press.) I don't think any of the people I fired like me any longer, but I like many of them. In fact, in only two cases did I fire someone I disliked or was angry with.

- **Do it right, but do it.** Don't wallow in helping people improve their performance, whether out of fear of litigation or guilt that you chose the wrong person or didn't help them improve. Fire faster.

You don't need a list of tips on how to fire: just imagine yourself doing a bad job and needing to be fired. Then treat your employee as you would like to be treated.

NINE

Niceties:
Manners and Rituals

I'T'S SIMPLE, ACTUALLY. MANNERS MATTER. MANY OTHER-wise smart people forget the niceties, and pay a price. I know that my good manners have helped me succeed in quantifiable ways. Yeah, I'm smart. Lots of people are smart. But good manners are an easy way to differentiate yourself. And there is no way for me to say this without sounding like an old fart, but so be it. In my thirty years in business, good manners have become increasingly rare. If you ignore every book, including this one, on developing your emotional IQ, or on how to execute, or on swimming with sharks, and just mind your manners, you are ahead of the game. Various business books for women (by Kate White and Lois Frankel, notably) have denigrated the "nice girl." I respectfully—nicely, politely—think otherwise.

Return phone calls and emails.

One exception to this rule: I don't answer emails or letters from vendors or supplicants who don't bother to find out that Robin can be a woman's name, or who misspell Wolaner.

Bernie Brillstein, in his terrific memoir, *Where Did I Go Right? You're No One in Hollywood Unless Someone Wants You Dead* (Little, Brown, 1999), puts it well: "Some people think manners have no place in business because it's one big power game. The less you care, the more you're in control. Bullshit. Why can't you be polite and still have power? Being polite stands out against the times you can't be—giving you more power. We all have to break someone's balls sometimes, but does that mean you can't write a thank-you note?" His viewpoint illustrates why I depart from the "antinice" school: If you *are* a decent, nice person, being yourself is both genuine and disarming. Acting less nice as a way to gain power is false and weak.

Returning phone calls and emails is my literal advice, but is also a metaphor for common courtesy and decency. And obviously you extend those courtesies to everyone, regardless of rank. Just as an executive can be judged by the behavior of his personal assistant, you can be judged by how you treat assistants. (And you can watch others' behavior toward underlings for vital clues to their character. This was Martha Stewart's undoing; don't let it be yours.) In addition to decency, it's practical: People move up.

Follow-up is easy and instills trust.

In 1985, I had just about exhausted my funds in trying to launch *Parenting* when I was introduced to Don Spurdle, a VP of magazine development at Time Inc. Don was Old Time Inc.—from a wealthy family, he'd gone to all the right schools. I was not someone whose background put him at ease. (To the extent he'd heard of *Mother Jones*, he later said, he assumed I would walk into his office with a marijuana joint behind my ear.) He explained that Time didn't let other people start magazines for them, but I could come to work on their project. I declined, politely. "Probably you will be a huge success and someday we'll buy you for an obscene amount of money," he said. I thanked him, gathered up my materials, and left his office.

Several months later, my funds were even lower, and my spirits along with them. At 6:15 A.M. the phone rang: "I work for Ruth Shields, the head of Time Inc. magazine development, and we've been working on a similar project to yours and were wondering if you would come to New York to talk about it." I was so sick of New Yorkers not bothering to think about the time difference that I was abrupt with the MBA on the line: "I've already met with Don Spurdle, and I don't have the time to waste meeting dozens of people at Time Inc."

Hanging up, my husband and I agreed that perhaps I should wait to have my coffee before answering the phone in the future, and I decided to check out this latest overture. I had two friends who worked—several levels down from Ruth—at Time, and put in calls to them. I also called Spurdle, as a courtesy, for I'd learned that he and Ruth headed rival departments of magazine development; I wanted to be completely aboveboard if I was now going to talk with his rival. Spurdle was out of the country, so I just left a message. I realize now that this simple display of good manners showed him that he could trust me, and that while our cultural backgrounds might be different, I probably wouldn't embarrass him. I hadn't yet learned about navigating the Byzantine hierarchy of a large, political company, but my parents had taught me good manners.

The next day one of my Time Inc. sources called to tell me that there had been a reorganization and Ruth was no longer in magazine development. I felt triumphant that I hadn't chased this false lead very vigorously, and went back to my conversations with other potential investors. A week or so later Spurdle called; he'd appreciated my touching base; he now ran the unified magazine development department; and he invited me to come back to New York for a chat, saying, "Although the chances of us doing a deal with you are less than one in a hundred, I can promise you a fast decision." He also offered to pick up my airfare. That was important. I only had enough money left to fund a few more fund-raising trips; the days when I drew a token salary were over; and I could see the day coming when I would again be drawing against my credit cards.

NAKED TRUTH #61

When in doubt about how to proceed, just rely on your good manners: You wouldn't spring an unwelcome surprise on a business partner; that's common courtesy. Simple, really.

The Spurdle episode was a turning point in my life, but there were many other times when good manners led to good business outcomes. One was in a big test for *Parenting*: Our editors had assigned an article on the poor safety record of minivans, which at the time were held to the safety standards of trucks, not of passenger vehicles. In 1987, this was our biggest advertising category, so we were putting the very future of the magazine in jeopardy, but if reader safety were at stake, it was something we had to do. I put the editor-in-chief through a lot of second-guessing, making sure we had crossed every T in the story. Then the advertising team got on the phone to our clients, making sure they knew the story was coming and giving them the opportunity to withdraw their ads from the issue. While they may have moved out of that issue, because of the professionalism of the staff we didn't lose a single advertiser. The risks were high, but good manners trumped the downside. And I like to think we contributed to the pressure that led the manufacturers to change to car safety standards soon thereafter.

Manners came in handy again, after the sale of *Parenting* to Time Inc. I continued to run the magazine, and became head of magazine development as well. By 1991 I had been working with or for Chris Meigher for five years. Then two bitter rivals at Time Inc.—Chris and Bob Miller—exchanged jobs, and I had a new boss. Although new bosses happen in business all the time, it is more rare to begin reporting to an avowed enemy of the person you've been identified with. Whether that is the case for you or not, when you get a new boss, mind your manners!

I barely knew Bob: The enmity between the men was such that you were either a Meigher or Miller person, but my first impression, several years earlier, had been intriguing. I'd been in an elevator at a publishing convention and a handsome man in what appeared to be extremely expensive silk pajamas entered. I saw his name tag and introduced myself to Bob Miller. He certainly didn't look like the other Time Inc. executives. Bob and I chatted. I was immediately struck by his sense of humor and ease; as tightly wound as Chris was, this man was his opposite.

It is not in my nature to worry about self-preservation, so unlike other "Meigher people" I immediately called Bob to welcome him to TIV. My manners paid off, because he liked me immediately—although later that fondness led him to promote me to CEO of Sunset, a job for which I was ill-suited and vice versa.

NAKED TRUTH #62

Send thank-you notes (can be by email for little kindnesses) and condolence notes (always handwritten).

My mistakes in the manners area nag at me because they are so avoidable. An early introduction to serving on a board of directors began with a mistake. While I ran Sunset, a man identifying himself as the founder of The Territory Ahead catalog asked me for a meeting. Thinking he was a potential advertiser, I agreed. We had a very pleasant conversation, and then he told me the real reason for the visit: Dick Munro, former Time Inc. chairman, had recommended me as a board member who could help in his dealings with his partner Lands' End, based on my success in doing that with Time. Though I was attracted to this opportunity, the company—of which I am still a happy customer—was based in Santa Barbara, and I couldn't bear the idea of the prop jet I would need to fly on to attend meetings. I declined the invitation.

The mistake was that I never wrote to Dick Munro to thank him for the flattering thought; not only was it bad manners, it was bad business. Needless to say, he never referred another board opportunity to me, and I don't blame him. Dick, if you are reading this, please forgive my slip. All board opportunities are welcome.

GOOD, BAD, AND UGLY EXITS

Handling an exit properly will test your manners and self-control. I am very proud of the way I left *Parenting*, Sunset, and CNET. While two of the exits were of my own choosing, and one was imposed on me, in all cases I made sure to follow a few principles:

1. **Stay positive.** As a departing CEO, I let employees know—in personal talks, in emails, in group meetings—my confidence in the business and in my successor. Whatever reservations I had, I shared only with those higher up in the corporation (or with the board).

2. **Closure matters.** Ceremonies are important. Even if I now have more mementos than shelves to store them on, coworkers need closure when a leader leaves. I have given parties for people I have fired, to recognize their service to the company. It's sincere—although their recent contributions may have been wanting, their earlier years had many accomplishments—and much appreciated, by those leaving as well as staying.

3. **Keep your word.** Often in a leave-taking the public story is not completely truthful; certainly it wasn't when I left Sunset. But I made a deal, one that was best for the company, and I kept to it, even though it would have made me feel better to have told the truth.

4. **Take time.** When I am mentally done with a job I want to be out of there instantly. But it's important that the transition be done on a schedule acceptable to the company, and I did that even when I felt like a lame duck. Bad leave-takings remind me of the importance of a good one.

5. **Reach out.** If there is anything ambivalent about the terms of your departure—if you're leaving for a stated resignation, to "pursue other interests," or even the usually spurious "spend more time with my family"—it's important to let your

network of contacts know two things: They need the details of how to reach you, of course, but they also need to know what to expect if they call. Especially people within your company, who will feel awkward about calling if they may run into bitterness about their employer. For outsiders who don't know what to say to a potentially devastated person, telling them that you are okay and positive opens the door for them to call you, which in turn opens the door for networking your next move. This may feel phony, but save your venting for your closest friends who don't work in your industry.

I was hurt—unwarrantedly—by various friends who didn't contact me when news of my departure from Sunset made the *New York Times;* when I mailed them a letter with the press clipping and my contact info, and a few sentences on my cheery state of mind, I was flooded with support. I have held the hands of shell-shocked fired friends and forced them to write this kind of letter, and seen great job offers, and improved outlooks, result.

TEN

Tools of the Trade

M Y FELLOW WOMEN EXECUTIVES AND I HAVE LEARNED
a lot—the hard way. This chapter is the easy way. Sit
back and feel free to use or learn whatever you want from our
best practices.

Raising Money

It is excruciating to ask for an investment when all you have
is an idea backed by your résumé and some supporting docu-
ments. If I ever have to do it again, I will remember some
lessons from my experience with *Parenting*:

1. **Say yes to credit cards.** Before you quit your job to work
   on your dream (or just after you've quit—there's a lag
   before your new status is known), accept every offer you
   get in the mail; work on any bank relationship you have to
   get a line of credit. Thank you, MasterCard: your 18

percent interest rate was cheaper money than my seed investors'.

2. **Double time.** It will take longer than your worst estimate; make sure you budget for that.

3. **Timing is everything.** You never know. One prominent venture capitalist with publishing experience turned me down because of his lack of interest in magazines generally and the parenting market specifically. He then became a competitor by buying *Baby Talk*. He hadn't lied to me; he had changed his mind. Follow up on every lead. Go back to people who turned you down if they left you an opening, any reason to hope, or if circumstances have changed.

4. **Take no for an answer.** But don't let the person off the phone, or out of the room, until he or she has suggested other potential sources of funding. Over the long run, developing great relationships is more important than securing a check. And having trusted supporters will always make it easier for you to get access to funding when you need it.

5. **Don't make it even more personal.** Don't look for money from friends and family unless they are really, really rich. It's better for any angel investor to be able to lose their seed money without pain; if I were getting an investment from someone close to me personally, I would make sure it was an amount trivial to him or her. This is especially important, because later stage, larger investors tend to trample all over the seed investors.

6. **It's not fungible.** Don't take the money just because it's green. Bad partners haunt you.

7. **Don't start without it.** It's hard enough to raise money; don't do it with a must-make-payroll gun held to your head.

Start with two years' worth of capital, if at all possible. You'll burn it in one.

8. **Be on the same page as your investor.** Having goals in alignment is important; if your investor is looking for a quick return and your timeline is longer, or if they want less risk and you want to maximize the upside, you will have a problem.

9. **Don't let venture capitalists string you along.** VCs only take a long time to deliberate when they are going to turn you down. Move on first.

10. **Valuations are temporary.** I have seen start-ups go unfounded because of a founder's insistence on a particular valuation. (I was asked to help a founder with a promising dot-com concept in 1995; as I went through my Rolodex I found he had already approached everyone I knew. "They offered a low valuation" was his repeated answer. I put away the Rolodex, knowing he would never get started.) Other founders choose the wrong investors because of a different initial valuation, ignoring issues of alignment and control. Serious investors will make sure the management team has enough incentive. It's impossible to predict the course of a business in the first round of financing, and getting hung up on a valuation that will shift is silly.

How to Be a Better Public Speaker

Women have different tipping points as to when the size of the audience increases past what you would consider a presentation, turning it into a speech. Whether that point is two or eight or twenty, if your career is going well it will happen to you. Few women are immediately comfortable with public speaking. Here are the ways we've gotten better at this important skill.

The first moments: Although I am generally at ease in front of an audience, I don't leave that to chance. My opening remarks are scripted and written, so if I am nervous at first, I can get into a rhythm through reading. (I never read more than a few words, but I feel more secure knowing they are there.)

Find your sweet spot: Hilary Schneider gets the audience on her side: "I'll tell a vignette about my kids, or reveal some of my insecurities. Show that you are frank, honest, and human." As the female CEO of Marimba, a high-profile technology company in the nineties, Kim Polese found herself getting a "ridiculous" number of invitations. She was afraid of public speaking: "I had to really believe in what I was talking about. I needed to say something of substance, not just promote my company. I got a speech coach to help me on content—not on my style or vocalization. Saying something of substance gave me the confidence to be up there with people who had a cadre of speechwriters. I wrote my own keynotes."

Don't go last. Most moderators are incapable of keeping panel participants to the allotted time, and there is nothing worse than preparing for a panel discussion and being preempted. I would say anything in the advance planning, to the point of being considered rude and demanding (manners don't matter much if you are never going to see the moderator again) to avoid a repetition of the two times I've flown to a city and not been able to speak because of inept moderation.

The worst public-speaking sin: Many speakers, particularly those with oversize egos, don't consider what the audience is there to hear. By showing the courtesy (manners again matter) of tailoring your remarks for the audience's particular interests, you will get them on your side quickly. The funniest example I saw of a speaker failing to do that was Jim Clark, a founder of Netscape, who spoke before an audience of a few hundred women executives and repeatedly referred to "the guys" who built Netscape. Predictably, the first question from the audience was about whether women played any role at Netscape. He launched into an explanation of why there were so few women: because it was a technology company, mostly engineers who wanted to work around the clock. Stony silence, including from the women engineers on the panel who followed his keynote. He then went on to point out that his daughter was an engineer, but she had to leave the company when she married another employee. Stonier. Then he mentioned the high-ranking women: general counsel and human resources. The applause was barely polite.

Better than taking a class. Carol Smith took classes to overcome her fear of public speaking. "They don't work unless you immediately start giving speeches daily. Inderal—a beta blocker—is what violinists have used for years so their hands don't shake. If more people knew about it there would be no public speaking classes. Now I can really give a good speech, even though I still get nervous."

What to Do When You're In Over Your Head

If you are the only person at your company doing your particular job, and you're clueless, where do you turn? Usually not to your boss.

Ask vendors. I always found vendors to be an invaluable help. They already know a lot about your company—often more than you do—so admitting problems can make them allies. I learned this at *Runner's World,* where I had just barely learned the basics of newsstand sales when I was promoted to also run subscriptions (my main qualification being that I was shorter than the CEO). The account manager at Neodata, the fulfillment house that managed our subscription list and that of many other magazines, welcomed me to my new job with the words "*Runner's World* is considered out of control. I can help you."

Go to the top. When you are feeling vulnerable, it's hard to cold-call someone you don't know, but often the most powerful people have the most willingness to help. Kim Polese comments, "I kept thinking, 'Gotta find a mentor. There must be someone wiser than me that I can hook up with.' Maybe that person exists, maybe not, but I couldn't wait. I needed to get lots of smart people for their collective wisdom. When I was a product manager at Sun I called Vinod Khosla, one of Sun's founders. I found him, and lots of other prominent people I called, very willing to provide input."

Connect with friends. Even if they aren't expert in your field, your friends can give you the emotional support you won't get at work. Karen Behnke was agonizing over whether to go into private equity, a man's field, when a male friend commented, "'What are they going to do to you? Push you out of a third-floor window on Sand Hill Road?' I thought that image was so funny, I stopped worrying about it."

Fake it until you make it. P. K. Scheerle worked as a nurse at night while starting her business as an outsourcer of nursing services. She finally got a morning appointment to see a hard-to-reach nun who ran one hospital; arriving without sleep in her bloodied scrubs, she fell dead asleep in the waiting room. When the nun arrived she gently suggested rescheduling for another time, but P.K. insisted on the meeting—and got the business. "Nuns running hospitals were early role models for women. We got to be close, and she told me, 'Fake it until you make it. Never let them see you bleed. The more scared you are, the more confidence you show.'" Elsewhere in this book I advocate showing honest emotion; fear, however, is not usually a good emotion to share.

Better Decision Making

When a choice is difficult it's probably because both alternatives are close. I would rather risk a mistake than be indecisive, which is always a mistake. Valli Benesch agrees: "Sometimes you might not want to make a decision because it's tough, but indecision is worse." Karen Behnke warns, "Every time I have not followed my intuition, it's nailed me. Whether it's not firing someone fast enough or another decision, I know now I have to listen to my intuition."

When making a decision in crisis conditions, double-check your assumptions. Anne Bakar learned that lesson: "Bank of America was our longtime bank—Dick Rosenberg, the former president, was at my wedding. They were sold, but I thought we were fine. We were doing a deal in Oregon, and they pulled the rug out." How did she respond? "I saved that deal. We'd been told that it *had* to close in that week. Right from the beginning of negotiations, the timing was inflexible. When B of A pulled out, I couldn't make the deadline. I just picked up the phone to the Oregon official. I leveled with him and asked if there was any opening. Sometimes your key people will tell you things that are honest from their point of view, but they can have a limited perspective. The deadline moved." Desperate for financing, she continued to question underlying assumptions. "I called the seller and asked if they would take back a note. They did. You don't know if you don't ask."

Don't be shy about asking elementary questions. For a year or two, Time had supported one of its senior editors while he worked on a plan for a magazine for African-Americans. There were significant misgivings about whether ownership by Time Inc. would be an insurmountable obstacle to such a launch. I was asked to come in to discuss this with a few senior executives (but without the editor). They had obviously had many discussions on the topic, and brought me up to date. The basic concept was not dissimilar to *Parenting,* and in fact the business plan was based on that: As we were to *Parents,* this magazine would be to *Ebony. Ebony* was behind the times, dated, dumbed down. This made sense to me. I asked to see a copy of *Ebony.* The execs looked at each other and squirmed. No one—in the months they had been discussing and investing in this concept—had thought to look at a copy of *Ebony.* The idea died a quiet death soon thereafter. I've never been afraid to ask the most obvious question.

Set a deadline for making the decision. Hilary Schneider follows George Soros: "When he goes into a country, his analysts do the work and he stays just twenty-four, or maybe it was forty-eight, hours and makes a decision. More analysis is not going to help; he needs to listen to his gut. Setting a fast deadline will help you go with your gut. Just do it. If you have the right team you'll be right 87 to 90 percent of the time and hope the mistakes aren't too big."

The Best Negotiating Tips

Arthur Dubow once told me, "It's only losers who spend time during a negotiation worrying that the other side is getting too much. Focus on what you are getting, and whether it works for you." Truer words were never spoken. Bernie Brillstein quotes himself along a similar line: "Never look to the left, never look to the right. Look at your own career. If you're doing okay, you don't have to give a shit about anyone else. Tend to your own business and you'll do fine."

Laura Scher of Working Assets is an amazing negotiator: "If you don't ask for something, you won't get it. You can even negotiate when things are going down: If a corporate partner is relying on consistent numbers, preventing a drop can be more powerful than promising growth."

Jan Brandt is relentless, and the best negotiator I know. Jan became famous as the founding marketing director of AOL, when she realized that the service needed to be demonstrated to prospective customers by sending them a disk. She followed this marketing insight with a keen sense for establishing leverage at the beginning of a negotiation: "With vendors you can bluff. When I came to AOL we were paying $1.19 per disk. I didn't know anything about disks, but I thought, 'I bet these kids are being ripped off.' The vendor immediately came down to 99 cents, so I knew there was more there. I pitched a tantrum. 'The grown-ups are now in town; you should be ashamed of what you have been charging this company. Sharpen your pencils. You send this company a check for $150,000 as a rebate on your overcharging or I am not even going to entertain your bid. That's your cost of entry.' Then when they called, I had instructed my secretary to call to me, as if I was in the hall, without putting them on hold, so they could hear me ask her if they'd sent the $150K before I took their call."

Whether or not she had the upper hand in a negotiation, Jan understood the need to signal the end of the back-and-forth, and used drama and symbolism to do so. When she ran a direct-marketing agency specializing in nonprofits, "Greenpeace was negotiating and they were mad about something we had done. We were haggling back and forth, and finally I said, 'I have nothing more to give,' and stabbed my finger with the paper clip I was holding, drawing blood. They were scared and finished the deal." That wasn't her only war story. "I had been negotiating hard with this guy who wore really beautiful, expensive ties. I finally had the price I wanted and he said, 'Okay, do we have a deal? You have gotten everything you have asked for.' I said, 'I want your tie.' He thought I was kidding, but I wanted him to understand what my business was worth to him. Finally he asked if he could have it cleaned before he sent it to me, and I agreed."

ELEVEN

The Unbalanced Life of a Working Mother

T HE FIRST QUESTION I AM ASKED BY BUSINESS-SCHOOL audiences is, "How could you start a magazine for parents when you weren't one?" When I respond that I couldn't have started *Parenting* if I were a new mother, I have seen female students wince. But starting a business—working from when you wake up in the morning till you go to sleep, being willing to hop on a plane with six hours notice when a funder agrees to meet with you, to be on the road for weeks at a time—is not compatible with the kind of mother I or any women I've ever known want to be.

You can have it all, you just can't have it all at once.

If I had had children, *Parenting*'s first issues would have been better, because I would have known firsthand what the reader wanted. And I would have been more promotable to television talk shows, most of whom wanted the magazine founder to be a mother, like the audience. But I barely had the emotional reserves to handle a high-profile start-up at the same time as my father's cancer diagnosis and death and the disintegration of my marriage. If I'd had children, there is no doubt the magazine wouldn't have been possible with me at the helm.

NAKED TRUTH #63

You can't time your baby's conception. This will prepare you for giving up control, which is a side effect of parenthood.

After the magazine had been sold and well established, I remarried. At thirty-eight, I knew from reading every word of *Parenting* that it would take on average a year to get pregnant. Six months after I became CEO of Sunset, my best friend Peggy visited us for the holidays and New Year's Eve, but I got the flu and wasn't much company. It's because of that flu, coinciding with our New Year's resolution to try to get pregnant in 1993, that I can precisely date the conception of my first child: January 2. So much for timing the pregnancy. Not for the last time, my knowledge about childbearing from *Parenting* would prove irrelevant.

My preconception view of pregnancy was simple: I would have an expanding belly for nine months, take six weeks off, and then return to work. I was very clear on the latter part—my experience with working mothers had been that if one took a longer leave, it was harder to separate from the baby. In fact, the short leave was the only thing I was right about.

I was immediately exhausted, and wanted to nap every afternoon. Worse than that, I didn't actually care very much about work, for the first time in my life. It didn't make sense: On the one hand, I did not entertain any thoughts of stopping work when the baby was born. I had no interest in taking a break from my career. But emotionally, for the first time, I didn't actually care about anything at work.

I hate admitting in print what I'd previously confided only to women friends who are mothers. But certainly my experience is not that of all, or even most, women. It was just mine. And it was not my experience with my second pregnancy. So my first experience of the quest for balance as a working mother was this: You can become unbalanced.

NAKED TRUTH #64

Get ready for people to act weirdly; it comes with the pregnancy territory.

Most pregnant women can share stories about odd behavior—the stranger on a bus rubbing your belly, unsolicited advice on your meal. It's as if your changing profile throws off others' sense of boundaries, and this can be especially off-putting in the office. While men have mainly learned how to work with us breast-featuring creatures, our pregnant bellies can throw them for a loop. It's an opportunity for breaking down boundaries, for better or worse, as your female status becomes impossible for them to ignore. Female bosses are trickier: The childless ones are usually very self-conscious and hide any negative reactions; the mothers expect your pregnancy to be just like theirs but are generally sympathetic.

I was Time Warner's first pregnant divisional CEO, and no one quite knew how to react.

Jerry Levin's reaction discomfited other people, but I loved it. I happened to be in New York for our mutual birthday, and dropped off an armful of flowers at his newish Rockefeller Center digs. He was out that day—at a Mets game with his son—but the next day his assistant tracked me down and asked me to drop by whenever I had a chance. Even though it was interrupting a closed-door meeting with several people I didn't know, she ushered me in. Jerry said, "I just wanted to rub your belly," which he proceeded to do before showering me with Bugs Bunnies and other Time Warner tchotzkes for the baby and me. I was giddy with the feeling that I really could be a pregnant CEO. No problem.

NAKED TRUTH #65

Men try to protect pregnant employees and end up doing the opposite.

I remember studying in my industrial relations college the question of whether workplace rules setting stricter safety standards for pregnant women and women of childbearing age were discriminatory. Intelligent people can disagree on whether special treatment is progressive or regressive, but I can testify that alleged concern can be as noxious as exposure to fumes. I thought I had taken care of the most pressing business problems at Sunset before taking maternity leave. I told everyone to leave me alone for two weeks after the delivery. Fifteen days after Terry's birth the phone rang with alarming news. I conferred with Sunset's CFO, followed up with some of the advertising salespeople on my own, and concluded I needed to fire two of my top managers. I called Bob Miller to tell him of the problems, and he said, "I know." I sputtered, "How could you know and not tell me?" And he replied, "I didn't want you to be worried during your leave." Because of his misplaced discretion my leave was consumed with a firing and a publisher search.

I can't fully blame Bob, or even my raging hormones. I had been so determined to wrap up every loose end before my leave that I had blinded myself to bad news. If you can begin the process of letting go of perfection before you give birth, you will be better prepared for the imperfections that come with the job.

Don't count on men, or most women, to look out for you during your pregnancy and leave. If there was ever a time to be resolute in your self-benchmarking this is it, but you also need to forgive yourself. Be aware of where you are not up to your usual snuff, and do your best. This is great practice for being a mother.

NAKED TRUTH #66

Bring all your best business practices to hiring a nanny. They are more important than vice presidents or senior managers, and harder to fire.

An even more important hire was one I was less qualified to make: the nanny. We needed someone who could be paid on the books. Beyond that, I had a few preconceptions. After interviewing a bunch of women who had posted signs on a local parents' bulletin board, we hadn't found anyone. (My active-listening skills proved invaluable. We almost hired a woman, and as usual in my interviewing, I let her talk and fill the silence, until she bragged about her success potty-training a one-year-old; my technique saved us from a rigid disciplinarian.)

There was a lot of publicity about an English nanny in Boston who had been tried for killing an infant she had allegedly thrown against a wall. I was convinced that her acquittal was more a jury punishing a working mother than a testament to her innocence, and terrified that I would miss the signs of a killer. Siobhan McGuinness was not what I was looking for: Only twenty years old, with just one nonfamily reference, she was honest in telling us that she planned to return to Ireland in five years. And she admitted she wasn't a cook. I was hoping for a gourmet who would commit to us until Terry started college. When I asked if she would accompany Terry and me on business trips, she said she wouldn't; after she left the interview and, I later learned, conferred with her fiancé, she called back to say she would be willing to travel. That honesty, and her desire for the job, impressed me, and she laughed at my husband's jokes. Some sense developed from all the hiring I've done stood me in good stead: We hired Siobhan, the best decision we've ever made as parents.

I couldn't tell her my fears. But they were soon dissipated. Steve would return home during the day to find Terry asleep on Siobhan's shoulder as she held a book in the other hand. When Steve urged Siobhan to put the baby down so that she could have a break, she said, "But I like to hold him." Within a few weeks I never had to worry whether Terry was in good hands—better than mine, I have always said (and, damnably, no one has demurred).

NAKED TRUTH #67

No one is a fully competent working mother.

As the founder of *Parenting*, perhaps I have a right to state this Naked Truth.

As a working CEO, perhaps it's self-defense. There will be many instances where a new mother feels incapable of doing anything right, whether it be presenting a nipple to the baby or presenting a strategic plan to the board. I have no magic bullet to offer you except wisdom gained in hindsight: Focus on the areas you do well, and forgive yourself for those you don't. Be vigilant in keeping your areas of competence uncompromised: Don't delegate the parts of your job in the office or at home that make you feel good. Celebrate your victories: When you manage to juggle the needs of your infant with those of your job, tell lots of people. Mainly you will be trying to hide the little defeats, so making noise when things work out is important.

At first, my return to work was a relief. At six weeks, Terry was oblivious to my absence, and I loved the freedom to go out to lunch and exercise my brain again. Then fatigue hit me. I am not sure I can convey how tired I was. Better writers have captured the exhaustion of the working mother of an infant. Nor do I want to give fodder to bigots who think that women should be penalized in the workplace because they don't function as well around childbirth. And I know how lucky I was: Terry wasn't particularly fussy. He just would wake up every couple of hours. If he didn't wake up, I would—and scurry down the hall to check on his breathing.

I would leave the house at 7:30 (before the nanny arrived) and try to get home by 6:30 when she left; this meant leaving work right at 5:30 and hoping. With the traffic problems in the Bay Area, I was often later than that, and would cry in my car. Some nights, when the traffic wasn't too bad, I would arrive in our garage and realize I had no consciousness of the last half hour. I guess I was awake; I didn't have an accident, but it couldn't have been the best condition for driving. I was continuing to nurse Terry, despite my lack of interest in the whole procedure. (And despite my childhood fantasy of owning a cow, I didn't enjoy being one.) I had determined to carry on for three months, and precisely on schedule I returned the pump to the rental place. I then realized that this was the one aspect of caring for this baby that I could do completely competently, and that no one else could—not Steve or Siobhan, both of whom had an easier time taking care of him. So I ended up rerenting the pump (they had never seen that before) and being a nursing mother for six months, much to my surprise.

The height, or nadir, of my breast-pumping experience came at an all-day meeting of the board of advisers to the U.C.-Berkeley School of Journalism, on which I sat for a number of years. The building was under renovation, and the single-occupant bathroom, which would otherwise have been perfect, was not totally complete: It lacked a doorknob. I managed to find a way to plug in the pump and stretch the cord to the door, where I sat on the floor with my back holding the door shut. I had barely stopped congratulating myself when all the lights went out. They were on a motion-detector. So I needed to half-rise every three minutes or so to wave my arms to put the lights back on. It was one of those experiences that made me feel I'd won some sort of battle.

Elizabeth Perle, in her book *When Work Doesn't Work Anymore,* captured the feelings of a mother at midlife perfectly: "On a good day, when the bills are paid, when I know I made brilliant points in the eleven o'clock marketing meeting, when I haven't been eating to deal with my anxiety and my son has slept through the night, I am the luckiest person on earth to be able to do all the different things that make up my life. I feel vital and powerful. I am invincible. On a bad day, when every minute part of my life has someone's or something's name written on it, I am sure I will go crazy and end up on top of a water tank with an Uzi if I'm asked a question as simple as 'Honey, have you seen my green tie?'"

NAKED TRUTH #68

The failure to achieve pregnancy is even more distracting and enervating than getting pregnant.

In 1997 I had one goal: to try to get and stay pregnant. At forty-three, my clock was ticking loudly (even though my ob/gyn assured me that I had the "hormones of an eighteen-year-old." All I could tell him was that those hormones sure felt different at eighteen). Although headhunters were calling with some regularity as Internet frenzy was in full swing, I couldn't consider committing to a CEO role. I figured that if

I couldn't have a second child, I would settle for a CEO job in a few years. The Internet would wait for me.

I had joined Young Presidents' Organization, an international group of people who'd become presidents before they turned forty-four. For the first time in my life I had a support group for people at my level in business; I had always had great girlfriends, but many were not businesspeople, and those who were tended to work with me, which restricted our conversations. My YPO forum had been an incredible source of support and friendship for me, and at this juncture became a kind of monthly fertility report: not pregnant, pregnant, miscarriage, etc. We called ourselves the Deep Forum and shared our innermost confidences with each other. One of my favorite members of the forum was Halsey Minor, the founder of CNET. Halsey was a decade younger than I, and his stake in CNET was worth over $100 million. Yet the company had stalled since going public in the summer of 1996 (making it one of the granddaddies of Internet companies).

I know that my situation in joining CNET was rare if not unique. It was a talent-seller's market; Internet companies were desperate for management. Yet I believe a few lessons can be learned from my five years there, on both sides of the Internet bubble.

I traded the glamour and accountability of the CEO slot to become an executive vice president. Although at first I reported to the CEO (until it was clear that cofounder and then-COO Shelby Bonnie and I were the true partners), I didn't have the ultimate responsibility; for the first time in over a decade, I was not in charge of sales. This made the job, during a grueling pregnancy, feel like a paid vacation. It's controversial to take a step back in your career: Conventional wisdom, and most business books, would say that I was "mommy-tracked" and took myself out of the running for CEO jobs. I suppose only time will tell, but my friends in the executive search field don't seem worried about my marketability. I definitely added skills to my portfolio.

One of the raging questions of our time, for women who view business as a lifelong occupation, is whether you can stop working completely and reenter years later. Before giving up on the stress of combining work and a new family, consider a lesser job. You keep learning, and earning.

This is easier to do when starting a job than midway through. As long as you are in the office at least 60 percent of the time (and the schedule is set by the business's reality, not yours), you can be as effective as a full-timer. When I joined CNET as a half-timer I realized that the pace of an Internet company was such that I needed to be in the office every day, from 8:30 to 5:30. That would sound like full-time, but I carved out hours for lunch with friends, online shopping/ other tasks, and errands of all sorts. It felt like I was always around to my colleagues, but I never put in more than thirty hours (and that is about half-time for a senior executive).

Only you can figure out the financial considerations in working part-time beyond the obvious. (On one side of the ledger: the expensive time-saving choices we make when pressed by a full schedule; on the other, no time for recreational shopping; on one side, need for manicures; on the other, no time for a gym membership; no time to monitor your investments, but maybe that leads to better performance.) Your ledger will look different from mine, but one thing we all have in common: It's worth any financial sacrifice to have the family life you want. That life is probably not that of Ozzie and Harriet, but it also probably isn't the dual career–obsessed couples we read about.

NAKED TRUTH #70

The workplace is a great source of friendship, especially for new mothers.

Despite all that has been written about the decline in loyalty to one's company, I believe that one's business colleagues make up one of the most important communities in most people's lives. Women can find an intense bond with colleagues who happen to be mothers of young children. Great camaraderie exists even, or especially, at companies that don't treat their workers well.

The feeling of belonging I got from my various workplaces was really important, after a lonely childhood. Some companies felt to me like family: Time Inc., despite its political, WASPy nature; *Penthouse*, despite its sexual content. Although CNET was the first time I would be older than my colleagues, playing the maternal role in the office felt familiar. And since working and having young children left little time for hanging out with my "personal" friends, those office friendships became even more important. What will feel familial to you will be different, as families are different, but that feeling is something to note whenever you think about changing jobs. Why aren't we comfortable admitting that a reason for staying in our jobs, or leaving them, is that our friends are there and we like to see them?

Although I can think of dozens of examples where men promoted unqualified friends, or allowed them to remain in jobs they performed badly, I can't think of any where a man lost or damaged an office friendship by telling the hard truth. I know many women who have. For me, those occasions remain painful to remember, but I would rather have a few instances of pain than have missed the opportunity to form lasting friendships over my three decades of work.

NAKED TRUTH #71

Try your best not to let work cause you to miss an important life event. When it happens, as it will, don't let it eat away at you.

My father's decline from cancer in the first year of *Parenting*'s life was rapid. My sister, Ellen, came to Florida on an emergency leave from London at Thanksgiving, when it became clear that her planned Christmas visit would be too late. Ellen's leave was set to run out in the second week of December. We decided I would go back to San Francisco to spend a week working so I could be there when she needed to go to London. My father died on December 4. I wasn't there, but I am glad Ellen was.

Although I have regrets about instances where I did

business instead of being with my father, I now know that continuing with the magazine was the right thing—not just for the employees, but also for my family. Its success was clear in 1987, and my father died knowing our family would be financially secure. He felt responsible in a superficial way for the magazine's inception. Back in the early 1980s, when I was working at *Mother Jones,* at a family dinner we'd gotten into a political argument. He turned to the assembled cousins and said, "When she worked at *Runner's World* she ran a marathon. I don't even want to think what she did at *Penthouse.* Now she's more left-wing than ever. When is she going to work for a baby magazine?"

Beginning with his diagnosis, until his death seventeen months later, most major developments in my father's illness necessitated my making a choice between being with my family and being at the helm of my new company. If you are faced with a similar balancing act—hopefully for happier reasons, like being a parent of a young child—the most important lesson is to be conscious of the decisions and trade-offs. Don't miss life events through inattention, and certainly don't make it routine. (Kids' firsts—word, step, haircut—seem momentous at the time, but aren't important or even clear: Was that a word? If so, what was it?) None of it should wrack you with guilt or, even worse, lose you sleep that you desperately need, and if it does that is a sign of either a bigger problem with priorities, or an overly developed sense of responsibility.

THE TRUTHS ABOUT WORKING MOTHERS

"Truths" is plural because of my fervent belief about combining family and career: Each woman's experience is unique. And all mothers work—whether paid or not. At the risk of gross generalization, here are some things I've learned—for me—from being a pregnant CEO and top executive. It's even tougher, although somewhat less visible, for less senior women.

- If planning to return to work, a short leave is better. It's much easier to leave a six-week-old infant than a six-month-old baby who recognizes you.
- When leaving a six-week-old baby, any job will feel like a paid vacation.
- A visible box of Saltines is a dead giveaway (to other mothers) that someone has morning sickness. Hide them unless you are prepared to go public.
- Don't be surprised when male colleagues stare into your eyes intently. It's not a new connection; they are just afraid to look at your belly.
- Spend as little as possible on maternity clothes. Be shameless about asking for hand-me-downs. You will hate every item by the time you give birth.
- *Operating Instructions* by Anne Lamott is the best book ever written on becoming a mother. Do not read it until after you give birth.
- If physically possible, work until the last possible minute. Otherwise, you will do crazy nesting things that waste time and money, like shopping for a comfortable chair.
- Be explicit about what circumstances would permit colleagues to contact you during your leave. If you leave it up to them, some will contact you on trivial items and others will leave you out of crucial decisions.

- If you can afford a nanny, pay on the books so that you will be less vulnerable if you need to fire her. It's the law, and it's also smart.
- "When they get old enough to care what their hair looks like, they will brush it." This tip is from Leslie Jacobs; a CEO and mother of two daughters, she is referring to the need to prioritize and recognize that none of us is perfect. "I felt guilty for years for not making every school event, though I was home for dinner every night. Then when I sold my agency my seventh-grade daughter said in horror, 'Don't tell me you're going to be one of those car-pool moms.'"

TWELVE

What's Next

WRITING THIS BOOK HAS CAUSED ME TO REFLECT MORE on business lessons than I did as I was learning them. I'm getting itchy to put them into practice, to do one last early-stage company *the right way*.

By the time you read this my daughter, Bonnie, will be in grade school and I will be thinking about my next company. At first I thought I might go into the online meeting/networking area. As I wrote this book, I got divorced. In the half-time when my kids are with their father, I've been kissing frogs and princes, mainly meeting them through online services. I did some consulting (mostly ignored) for Yahoo's personals service. It's a fascinating area, and one without a clear business model (beyond dating) at this point.

A venture capitalist friend (whom I met through a networking site) couldn't believe I was tempted by a recruiter for one of the "social" start-ups: "Robin, there's no business model." That's the point: I am a true early-stage person, and thrill to the idea of finding a business model, or creating a product to serve a market.

Here are the Naked Truths that will inform the choice and content of my next job and that I suggest anyone making a transition consider:

- **It's the people, not the product.** I have been passionate about technology, running, left-wing politics, babies— before any were important in my nonwork life.
- **Make the important strategic and staffing decisions in the first ninety days.** If I can't listen to my gut at this point in my career, I'll never be able to.
- **Become dispensable.** At some point in your career or in a particular job, if you have to work a lot of hours, either you don't know how to delegate or you are with a business that isn't healthy enough.

Networking is still an area in search of a business model. And I've had another idea, exactly twenty years since I had the "Aha" moment on *Parenting* described in the next chapter. It's every bit as good an idea as *Parenting*, and I am in some ways better equipped to launch a business: I've done it before; I am wiser (okay, older); investors are plentiful; and I know more people to fill a management team than I could hire, at least at first. I'm rereading chapter 11 on balance and trying to figure out how my ambitions for the new company fit into a life filled with my children, friends, and a new relationship. Stay tuned.

THIRTEEN

P.S.: How a Nonparent and Anticapitalist Raised Millions to Found *Parenting* Magazine

THIS HAS BEEN A BOOK OF LESSONS, BUT THE POSTSCRIPT is just me telling my story. Read it if you are curious, or think you might someday want to do a start-up. There are a few Naked Truths, but mainly just one truth: You don't have to fit the entrepreneurial stereotype to launch a successful business.

NAKED TRUTH #72

Be honest with yourself, if not with everyone else, about your motivation.

There's probably a successful entrepreneur who was driven purely by a desire for money; I just haven't met him yet. The desire for control is more common. Sometimes money is used as a scorecard, but it is secondary to the ultimate goal. Although I had long been fascinated by magazine start-ups, I had never aspired to do one myself. I thought entrepreneurs were driven, single-minded, almost maniacal; while I was interested intellectually in doing a magazine launch the right way, I didn't have the burning passion of company founders I'd read about. I'd known a few magazine entrepreneurs, and while Bob Guccione and Bob Anderson (founders of *Penthouse* and *Runner's World,* respectively), for example, couldn't be more different, they shared that intensity and self-conviction that I lacked. At the time, I didn't realize that intensity and conviction could grow.

After running *Mother Jones* for several years I certainly had more skills and experience than either Guccione or Anderson had had when founding their magazines. Having run a money-losing magazine I knew publishing economics inside out. Over the years I had developed a world-class network of talented pals. And although I didn't have an advertising background, my experience in editorial, circulation, and finance qualified me to tackle anything else that came along. All that I lacked was a clear sense that I really wanted to launch my own magazine. And millions of dollars. Oh.

The fact that at some level I was thinking about launching a magazine may have put me in the position to capture the idea when it came to me. (As Louis Pasteur said, Chance favors the prepared mind.) The "aha" moment emerged out of a number of ostensibly random events, all of which led to my moment of inspiration.

In 1984, I had helped create an on-site nursery at *Mother Jones.* Our new circulation director was five months pregnant when she interviewed with us, and we considered her the ideal candidate. Moreover, our advertising head and the office manager were also expecting. And so we converted a storage area into a nursery, with the working parents sharing the cost of a sitter.

It only cost a few thousand dollars, and I raised the money easily from vendors and sympathetic donors. I found that people were delighted to help working mothers. Another surprise came when the presence of babies in the workplace turned out to be exciting and wonderful—not the negative distraction I had imagined. All of us—the women considering babies themselves, like me, the men whose thoughts were elsewhere—took breaks and went to the nursery to inhale the smell of infants, to try to get a giggle out of them.

One November day I walked down to the circulation director's office and asked her, "So what magazine do you read now that you're a mother?" Fran responded, "Someone gave me a subscription to *Parents*, but it's really like *Ladies' Home Journal* and not for me."

Aha.

Fran was using shorthand, which I understood immediately. *Ladies' Home Journal* was one of the Seven Sisters—old-fashioned women's magazines (*Woman's Day, Good Housekeeping, Redbook*, etc.) that looked and read as if they were being edited in 1959. Their circulations were declining, although not as drastically as they did in later years, as they missed a new generation of women who took one look at their covers and thought, "My mother's magazine." *Parents* magazine advertised itself as "the Eighth Sister." Their management was not even smart enough to realize they were attaching their magazine to a sinking ship.

**The classic entrepreneurial myth is that
a charismatic founder has a brilliant idea and
instantly gives up everything to pursue his dream.
In fact, most successful entrepreneurs thrive by mitigating risk.**

After several years of teaching about start-ups at Radcliffe, I had an idea, and I was pretty sure it was a good one. As a card-carrying baby-boomer I was accustomed to noticing my friends' preoccupations and later reading about them as trends: It had happened with politics and running, just to mention two that coincided with my career moves. Now it seemed that everyone I knew was having a baby, or talking about having a baby. And they were parenting, or planning to parent, very differently from the last generation. The would-be fathers were determined to play more active roles than their fathers had. The mothers were determined to use their advanced educations to do the best possible job of motherhood.

I went home that night and as usual my husband was waiting for my arrival, with his list of questions about my day. He would write topics from the previous day into his Day-Timer, so he could be sure to follow up and show his interest.

I interrupted the questions. "I had an idea for a new magazine today. For both parents—but not old-fashioned like *Parents*, which is really just for mothers. I think that insults its readers. People today are raising kids differently, but there isn't a magazine for them." He put down his Day-Timer. Now his interest was real. Aristotle, his German short-haired pointer, could sense the change in tone and momentarily stopped chasing his tail. "This is great. You don't need to take a job, then; we can raise money and start a magazine." I couldn't believe he leaped to that conclusion immediately; I'd barely described the idea. "It isn't so easy. A consumer magazine takes a minimum of five million dollars. My background isn't perfect; these magazines have to carry a lot of advertising." He snapped his fingers with impatience. He didn't know the first thing about magazines, but he knew I did. "C'mon, sweetie, you've written a million business plans with your Radcliffe kids. That's what it takes to raise money. I'll make a list of all the people we know that we can ask." "And what will we live on while we raise that money?" This made him pause.

My husband was either greedy or a visionary, and assured me that raising millions would be no problem (although probably not from the investors whose money he had just lost in a failed gourmet food store), so the next day I gave three months' notice to *Mother Jones* and resigned. I decided that I would continue to look for a job while writing the business plan and raising money, so if the three months went by and the money for the magazine wasn't there, we would have something to fall back on.

While the literature paints the "aha" moment and the decision to attempt a start-up as one and the same, for many entrepreneurs there is a lot of soul-searching involved before committing. I believed in my heart that this venture could work, but in order to help make this decision I took the opposite tack of eliminating the reasons not to do so. I started to look for the Achilles' heel in the concept. They all have problems, and I secretly hoped this idea would prove bad. Then I could take a job and forget this impossible dream. I had such ambivalence about the venture, in fact, that when I interviewed for a direct-marketing position with Joan Barnes, the founder of Gymboree, I offered to sign on as a hired hand if she wanted to publish a Gymboree magazine. Fortunately, she said, "No."

And so it began. I know entrepreneurs often paint an exciting picture of the early days in a garage (or at a kitchen counter, in my case). Some of them even found the early days as exciting as the stories. I'm not one of them. Nineteen years later, my stomach still gets queasy when I tell the story.

NAKED TRUTH #74

If an idea is a good one, more than one person will have it. Don't freak out! Consider it a marketplace validation of your concept. Win through superior execution. It's not about being first, but about lasting.

My biggest fear at the time was that someone else would beat me to the punch. Every day that slipped by seemed to make it more likely that someone else would launch a magazine for this new generation of parents. I was not just being paranoid: The trade press had lots of mentions of various, better funded publishing people dabbling with this idea, from the founder of *American Health* to the publisher of *Cosmopolitan*. It was February 1985, and I thought I could get an issue out by January 1986, an excruciating delay.

One of *Mother Jones's* editors could barely contain his glee when he told me, "Oh, it sounds like you and Jeff Stein [a *MoJo* writer] are working on the same idea." Grimly, I called Jeff in Washington and we talked vaguely about the new way of parenting—it was no longer just about mothers— and about how bad *Parents* was. His team (team! It was just me so far!) had raised money for a test mailing and issue. I said, "It sounds like you are way ahead of me. Should we share our working titles so at least we don't call them the same thing?" Jeff said sure; theirs was called *Fathers*. I suppressed my giggles of relief and told him my working title was *Parenting*.

In fact, there were other people whose ideas were almost exactly the same as mine, and just as far ahead as the ill-fated *Fathers* team. The key to success is not to be obsessed by rivals, or reactive to their moves. Stay focused on what you need to achieve.

NAKED TRUTH #75

**Whatever amount of money you think it will take . . .
it will take double that.**

There are two types of entrepreneurs: those who thrive on money raising/deal making, and those who are suited to running a business. I am in the latter camp. If you are in the former, let me know, maybe we can do something. And if not with me, do yourself a favor and team up with someone who can actually run the business you get funded.

It infuriated me when investors said that the magazine launch would cost double my careful projections. They were right. That doesn't mean raise more—you probably can't, anyway—but think about what you'll do when you need more, and how it affects your choice of investors.

When I had the idea to start *Parenting* the conventional wisdom was that a national consumer magazine would take $5 million to launch. (I believe the current conventional wisdom is $20 million.)

It would be hard to imagine a person less qualified than I to raise money for *Parenting*. Not only had I never raised a dime before, but my leftish politics made me somewhat wary of people with wealth. Luckily, I had a friend who shared my politics but not my wariness. I was trying to interest Jeffrey Klein in becoming *Parenting*'s editor should I be able to raise the money. Jeffrey had been editor of *San Francisco* magazine in one of its many incarnations. A friend of his called in February and said, "I know a rich guy who is looking at buying *San Francisco*; can you talk to him?" Jeffrey talked with Arthur Dubow, a New York–based venture capitalist who was as much looking for a reason to visit San Francisco regularly as for an investment. "*San Francisco* magazine will never work. You should call my friend Robin."

"Capitalist" was not a term we at *Mother Jones* would use to someone's face, and Arthur was unlike anyone I'd ever met. We met at the Washington Square Bar & Grill, then a literary hangout. Arthur was tall, twenty years my senior, with a cowboy hat, white hair, and a stammer that belied his brimming self-assurance. He quickly let me know that he had been a major funder of the sixties movie classic *Putney Swope* as well as the first man on the board of the National Organization for Women. Both credentials meant a lot to me, although much else about Arthur—the prestige of his Georgica Pond address, various friends' names—was so out of my realm that I didn't know if he was as impressive as his bearing indicated. He believed that Harvard was the center of the universe, so my annual week teaching at Radcliffe seemed to impress him more than my various jobs in the publishing business.

I told Arthur I wanted to raise $100,000 to pay myself $27,500 for six months, plus the travel, legal, and other expenses (like buying a computer) of writing a business plan and prototyping the magazine. That in turn would give us the ammunition to raise $5 million for the launch. It dawned on me that the January 1986 date I'd promised myself for the first issue was a pipe dream, until Arthur asked questions about all the steps involved; I hadn't thought in terms of time. I knew everything that magazines involved; I just couldn't bear to think of how long it would take.

NAKED TRUTH #76

Vet your potential donors and partners vigorously— more vigorously than they check you out. They can survive the loss of their investment; your venture might not survive the interference of a bad partner.

At that lunch Arthur told me that he was probably in. He wanted me to discuss the plan with his friend Gil Kaplan, the founder of *Institutional Investor* magazine (best known for renting the New York Philharmonic so he could conduct). I wanted his money, but before I took Arthur's advice I went to *Mother Jones* writer/editor Mark Dowie (who owed me for luring me to *MoJo*) and asked him to use his investigative stealth and find out what he could about this man. After all, Mark had infiltrated Ford Motor Company to uncover their

Pinto problems. Two days later, Arthur called. "Are you having me investigated?" he demanded. Now it was my turn to stammer. He told me that no one looking for his money had ever thought to check him out, and he thought it showed I was smart. Whew.

Arthur sent me a check for five thousand dollars with a note saying it was "walking around money." Opening that envelope was one of the most thrilling moments of my life. My elation was tempered only slightly by Arthur's conditions, handwritten on the note accompanying his check: If I raised the rest of the seed money from qualified people ("no friends and family, no doctors or athletes") who could help on the larger fund-raising mission, he'd put in more. As I didn't know anyone who could risk the twenty-five thousand dollar minimum investment, I could live with Arthur's rule easily.

For the next few months, as I crisscrossed the country on Arthur's money looking for more, I was not exactly a stylish traveler. People Express would take me from Oakland to Newark. I usually stayed on my best friend Peggy's couch, often arriving from the red-eye for a nap as she headed to work. More comfortable digs came from Harry Quadracci, owner of QuadGraphics, *Mother Jones*'s printer. Quad's West Coast salesperson, Herb Siderman, told Harry of my plan, and Harry offered to let me stay in his New York apartment as long as other Quad employees weren't using it. This was a swank place at Park Avenue and East Fifty-seventh, and I am grateful to this day for Harry's belief in me. (A week after I wrote this paragraph in July 2002, Harry Quadracci drowned in the lake beside his home in Wisconsin. This good man had changed the lives of so many people, in ways both profound and small.)

I wasn't just fund-raising; I was also hunting for key

members of the management team while planning the direct-mail test that Arthur's friend Gil had insisted was necessary. (I had opposed this; I was sure I could pull off a successful direct-mail test, and that that wasn't the highest risk part of the magazine's launch. Besides, it added $100,000 to my budget.) Although I didn't want to spend the time and money on a direct-mail test, I trusted Arthur's view of what fund-raising would take, and revised my plans.

NAKED TRUTH #77

Entrepreneurs prefer mitigating a risk to taking one. A sure way to minimize the chance of failure is to enlist the support of a network of talented people.

What made me successful in this phase was the fact that I had so many talented friends from my years in the publishing business, and they were all willing to help me without pay, trusting that I would take care of them if and when I could. Jan Brandt, then head of a small direct-marketing agency, told me to look for lists of mothers of babies—the younger the better, pregnant would be best. Two of the top publishing consultants, who normally commanded high fees and would not normally collaborate, were at my beck and call—I had been a Radcliffe course teaching colleague of one, and a client of the other, and had kept connections to both. Because he'd been a West Coast publisher who shared many friends with me, the CEO of American Express Publishing clued me in on "big league" publishing compensation, and tutored me on advertising economics. The direct-mail package was designed by someone I'd dated. I think it's safe to say that no one ever started a publication with a better team of advisers; certainly no one ever got so much for free! The reasons I had this team have been covered in earlier chapters: I have good manners (I kept in touch even before email); I establish a favor bank before I need to draw on it; I am drawn to people more talented than I. If you are similar, you probably have, or are developing, a network of talent, too.

My career had never included any sales, and I had shied away from the fund-raising component of my *Mother Jones* job. Now I was asking for highly risky investments from people who didn't know me. All I had was a ten-page write-up of the concept, a budget, and my résumé.

I found this "dialing for dollars" phase excruciating. As I woke up, earlier and earlier because my sleep was so restless, I would become aware of my clenched stomach before I even looked at the clock. When in San Francisco my husband would goad me into making the calls, and I probably needed the push. I learned to call early or late in the day, when secretaries weren't around to screen me away from my targets. I would set deadlines to entitle myself to a reward—make three calls before I can have lunch or take a walk.

We wanted to drop the direct-mail test on August 31; missing that deadline would have meant waiting until December, the next safe window for direct mail, according to industry practice. I went as far as I could on Arthur's $5,000. I had $20,000 in credit card lines, and used it to make sure that if the rest of the money were raised, I would have a designed package ready to print.

Michael Todd, a brilliant art director, found the perfect photo to use for the envelope of the mailer: two young children, apparently brother and sister, facing away from the camera, clothed in yellow rain slickers, boots, and hats, looked into a drizzly gray Pacific ocean. It was so sophisticated and different from anything *Parents* would use: By not seeing the children's faces, any prospective reader could imagine them to be her own children, both beautiful and somewhat in need of protection. I know I did.

Everything in the package positioned the new magazine: "Finally, there's a contemporary magazine for parents . . . an exciting, informative, upbeat magazine for parents who want to grow along with their kids. Imagine a magazine that approaches parenting from your point of view, that shares your values, your interests, and your priorities. Imagine a magazine that understands that you didn't give up the other parts of your life when you became a parent. Imagine a magazine created by your contemporaries, people who aren't bound by old-fashioned presumptions and prejudices about how to raise children. Imagine a magazine that brings you information and ideas, not advice . . . that informs your decisions instead of trying to make them for you. Imagine a parenting magazine that takes for granted your intelligence, common sense, and sophistication. Until now you would have had to rely on your imagination alone to conjure up such a magazine. But not any more: PARENTING is here, and it's about time."

Well, *Parenting* wasn't exactly here, and time was running out.

NAKED TRUTH #78

Suspend disbelief. If your project was a good one before anyone turned you down, it still is.

I turned to friends for tips on how to keep up my morale, and they said things like the Naked Truth above. I needed the boosts. Although I had a few connections to money, only one of the ten investors who came through had met me before the excruciating fund-raising process had begun. (The positive view of this is that I raised the money from strangers, so if you lack connections, don't despair.)

I wrote a letter to Bob Guccione and Kathy Keeton, but never mailed it. I felt the association with *Penthouse* would not be good for a parenting magazine. However, my former boss Richard Smith was then head of circulation at *Playboy.* Christie Hefner had recently become CEO, and was both high profile and highly regarded. Arthur was convinced that others would follow the glamorous Christie in, and *Playboy* was more respectable than *Penthouse,* so I sent them the plan. Richard told me that they were in for $75,000 and suddenly the goal was in sight.

The agreement provided that I could start spending money on the direct-mail test, but not draw any pay, once $125,000 was committed. My goal was in sight: $75,000 from *Playboy,* $25,000 from Arthur, and I had four others I considered 50-50 shots, so the odds seemed in my favor for the first time.

NAKED TRUTH #79

No one is a committed investor until the papers are signed. While there are exceptions to this rule, behave as if it's universal.

Then Christie Hefner went on a several-week vacation to France, and her money guy told me that I had misunderstood; the commitment was only for $12,500, not the $75,000 Richard had told me. I was apoplectic—I wasn't even offering shares below $25,000. The *Playboy* guy was immovable, and Arthur and I decided it was better to take it than risk telling people that *Playboy* was now not in at all. I had to go back to the other committed investors, who rightly had felt that *Playboy*'s endorsement meant something at $75,000 but not at the pocket change that $12,500 represented. Several of the investors then chose to reduce to the new, $12,500 minimum. So just as I thought my fund-raising milestone had been hit, I was almost back at square one.

I had created the problem: By telling others that *Playboy* was in before I had signed paperwork, I now needed to explain their waffling, accept smaller investments than before, and allow a large corporation to get away with a piddling investment. (For years Christie Hefner referred dubious magazine startups to me, wasting my time and the entrepreneurs'.) I wish I had been able to tell *Playboy* to take a flying leap.

As tempting as it is, don't tell other potential investors that anyone is in until you know it for sure.

NAKED TRUTH #80

The time to arrange credit is when you don't need to borrow.

I took advice from a terrific ad salesperson: When my morale was too bad to get on the phone, I went to the movies. Or walked the dog. If you need to sell, you need to keep the smell of desperation away. Weeks of anxious days—interrupted by movies and dog walking—and sleepless nights went by, and I hit the $125,000 commitment and knew I could get the direct-mail package printed. This time my investors held firm. The first thing I did after paying back my credit card debt was to apply to raise the limits.

With the direct-mail test a smashing success, I tried to find the key members of the management team. I couldn't pay them (or myself), but identifying strong people would help raise the $5 million for the launch. A short time later, in a stroke of luck, I simultaneously found the editor and publisher for the launch.

For the publisher position I had begun calling media directors at advertising agencies, and from there compiled a list of possible candidates. One name appeared on two lists. Bob Cohen, my magazine consultant, told me I would either love her or hate her. Over lunch Carol Smith rattled off a list of bad career moves she'd made, while assuring me that she knew just how to sell a more affluent, educated version of *Parents*, a positioning she felt was akin to the one she had succeeded with when she'd launched *American Photographer*. (Oddly enough, Owen Edwards had worked on that launch as well; I could tell Carol was less than thrilled when I told her he would be the editor.)

Unlike most salespeople's positive spin on everything, Carol's frankness—self-deprecation, actually—made me pretty certain I'd found my partner. Somehow over that first lunch we figured out that we shared the same birthday. I don't consider myself superstitious, and I don't believe in astrology, but this seemed a good omen. I checked her out, and when I told her about the glowing things one publishing CEO had said about her, she responded, "If I respected his opinion that would be flattering." Now I was completely certain. Alan Bennett, the founder of *American Photographer*, reported, "Most advertising salespeople are in the business of inventing reality, so you never know if what they are telling you is true or self-delusion; Carol is painfully honest, and you will always know where you stand." Fortunately for me, Carol was then the publisher of *American Heritage*, which was in the process of being sold to Forbes, and could sit tight while I raised the rest of the money.

I was never in deeper over my head than when I began to raise serious money for *Parenting*. This is what it's like. You do the best you can. You try to minimize the external distractions, and be relentless about eliminating anything on your calendar that doesn't advance the cause. You need every brain cell, and all your emotional reserves, for the fund-raising process. Because although some fund-raising is more formatted than others, the process is never scripted. You need your wits, and your guts, about you.

Easier said than done, I know. In my case, I hadn't had the benefit of my own advice about arranging credit before I needed it, and was again facing the end of my resources. Although the direct-mail test had come in at budget, the seed phase had only contemplated a six-month period before the major funding arrived. At the end of 1985 I could no longer draw a salary and was stretching the last few thousand dollars to cover my frequent plane trips. Time Inc. might not have been promising, but I had to follow up on every lead.

When I arrived at the Time & Life Building for the first time on December 4, 1985, I was awed by its size: forty-six floors of offices devoted to magazines, each floor several times larger than any company I had ever worked for. But I was not expecting much from the meeting. As I sat in the waiting room Don Spurdle's secretary gave me a document to sign. It was a release, and to my eyes it sounded like I was giving them the right to steal my idea. I told the secretary that I needed to go to the bathroom and fled to the ground-floor lobby and called my lawyer, John Erickson, back in San Francisco. I read the release to him and John said, to my surprise, "It's cheaper for Time Inc. to buy your idea rather than steal it from you," he said, adding, "I'd rather sell shares in a lawsuit against Time than in a magazine start-up. Don't worry, Robin, this is not the kind of company that is going to steal your ideas." John knew more than I about the new territory I had entered, but I give myself credit for knowing to call him.

If I had asked for changes in the release form, or refused to sign it, even if Don Spurdle had gone ahead with a meeting (and he probably wouldn't have), our chemistry would have been altered, perhaps fatally. I would have been marked as naive or difficult.

I met with Don, his boss Chris Meigher, and assorted other people (meetings at Time Inc. were typically crowded affairs), all of whom asked questions that effortlessly showed more knowledge of magazine publishing than I'd seen in months of talking with potential investors. It still seemed inconceivable that anything could work out, but in that meeting something in me changed: I now wanted Time as a partner and was convinced *Parenting*'s chances of success would be enhanced by having knowledgeable partners, not to mention the clout of an industry giant, behind it.

The whole thing still seemed like such a long shot that I could keep my hunger for the deal totally submerged and present myself as someone with lots of other options. I had to fake the self-confidence part; what I didn't need to fake was my conviction that Time could not launch a competitive title with the agility and talent of my management team. Wow. It felt good to feel like I had a team.

Time began its due diligence, which mainly consisted of meeting with Owen and Carol, both of whom were known to Time. I was now in New York every other week, lunching with Don at overpriced restaurants near the Time & Life Building and going over my assumptions with various magazine development staffers.

In February the VCs formally turned me down, saying that the "risk/reward ratio" was not sufficient, and besides, they didn't understand magazine publishing (something they could have told me months earlier).

Now Field Publications was my only live prospect other than Time. They seemed serious, sending a few people to San Francisco to pore over my plans. (An unexpected but good outcome of that day was that Spurdle called and I couldn't take the time to talk to him, signaling that I did have other irons in the fire.) They ultimately declined to invest, and it wasn't until years later that I learned that a primary reason was concern over the impact of my husband's presence on the venture.

As earlier chapters make clear, ultimately Time Inc. invested $5 million for 49 percent of the venture and the right to buy my interest if the magazine succeeded. Today *Parenting* has a circulation of over two million—almost quadruple the size projected by my business plan.

I wrote this chapter as a postscript so that the majority of readers, who would never consider the white-knuckle days of a start-up, could easily skip it. If you've gotten this far, perhaps you are as crazy as I was. You need a little craziness to start something from scratch. If you read the chapter thinking, "I could have done this a lot better than she did," you are probably like the classic male entrepreneur, and more power to you. But if you read it thinking, "I don't have her connections, I would never have as good an idea, I couldn't take that kind of rejection," welcome to the world of the unlikely female entrepreneur. We don't think we are perfect for the job, but somehow we do it. And all power to you.

S INCE ACKNOWLEDGMENTS ARE THE FIRST THING I READ in other people's books, perhaps it's understandable that I started writing this section before finishing the rest.

Three people were the most involved in the project before Simon & Schuster arrived: Daniel Greenberg, agent extraordinaire, proved my theory that in choosing between a big name and a rising star, go for someone with ambition and energy. I am happy I did. Ron Kraft and Tom Ehrenfeld, who worked in different phases as editors on this project, were unstinting in their help and morale boosting.

Doris Cooper, my editor at Fireside/Simon & Schuster, is a tremendous talent who convinced me that her vision for this book was better than my original attempt. She is funny, smart, and driven—what a surprise that we clicked immediately, and kept clicking through many revisions. I am especially happy that Fireside is headed by a woman—and, in

Trish Todd, one whom I admire. Marcia Burch was always helpful on public relations.

My greatest business success came with more help than one has a right to expect from talented friends. The same was true in writing this book. I am in awe of the generosity of my amazing circle.

Friends who know much more than I do about writing read the manuscript and offered terrific, usually diplomatic, feedback: Richard Snow, Adam Moss, David Sheff, Lori Schryer, Liz Perle.

Sara Nelson did all that and more: educating me on book publishing, opening doors with agents and publishers, and in general (and as usual) being a wonderful friend.

Friends who lived the story with me gave great reality checks and not always gentle feedback: Carol Smith, Jan Brandt, Candy Meyers, Peggy Hamilton, David Markus, Eileen Rivkin, Jeffrey Klein.

Dianne Snedaker, my comrade in reentry into dating at midlife, was my most conscientious (and helpful) reader. Adair Lara is an amazing teacher—if you don't get a chance to take a writing course with her, as I did, do the next best thing and read one of her books. I enjoyed encouragement, ideas and/or feedback from Stewart Alsop, Michael Castleman, Melissa Houtte, Art Kern, Bill Marken, Susan Maruyama, Brianne Miller, Joe Nocera, Bob Nylen, Bruce Raskin, Susan Sachs, Amy Schoening and Lorraine Shanley.

The men and women of Young Presidents' Organization taught me so many of the lessons contained in this book— take it from someone who'd never joined anything before: If you qualify for membership, YPO is a sure way to be a better leader. Many members helped, and some are quoted in the book: especial thanks to my dear friends David Martin, Tony Brenner, Mary Ann Byrnes, and Nancy O'Neill.

I had it easy as a working mother, thanks to the best parenting decision that Steve Castleman and I made: bringing Siobhan McGuinness into our lives. I will always be grateful for the six years I spent working without worrying for a minute about my children's well-being.

Speaking of mothers, mine was a careful, if wincing, reader of the manuscript. She bears no responsibility for my romantic adventures, or for the title of this book, which she hated. However, if I can write, the credit goes to Harriet Wolaner Thaul.

Finally, there is a long list of people who taught me that the workplace is a great source of love, laughter, or learning—sometimes all three. You know who you are, and I am grateful to know all of you.

ROBIN WOLANER began her career as a copywriter at *Penthouse*, where she coined the famous slogan, *"Penthouse, more than just a pretty face."* The founder of *Parenting* magazine, she is a former vice president at Time Warner, where she launched *Vibe* and helped develop *Martha Stewart Living*. In 2003, Wolaner left her executive position at CNET Networks to write. She lives in San Francisco, California, with her two children.